A Time Has Come

the antichrist revealed

Ron Cameron

A Time Has Come
the antichrist revealed

ISBN-13: 978-0-692469-04-0

Order Online through Amazon.com

Follow on:
TWITTER: @roncameron777
FACEBOOK: facebook.com/ron.cameron.us
www.roncameron.us
ron.cameron.us@gmail.com

The author is available for radio, television, speaking engagements, print and online interviews.

Please contact the publisher: shorepublications@yahoo.com.

Published by Shore Publications
in the United States of America, 2016

Edited by: Marci McGuinness, Brynn Cunningham and John C. May

DEDICATION

To Marilyn, for my inspiration.

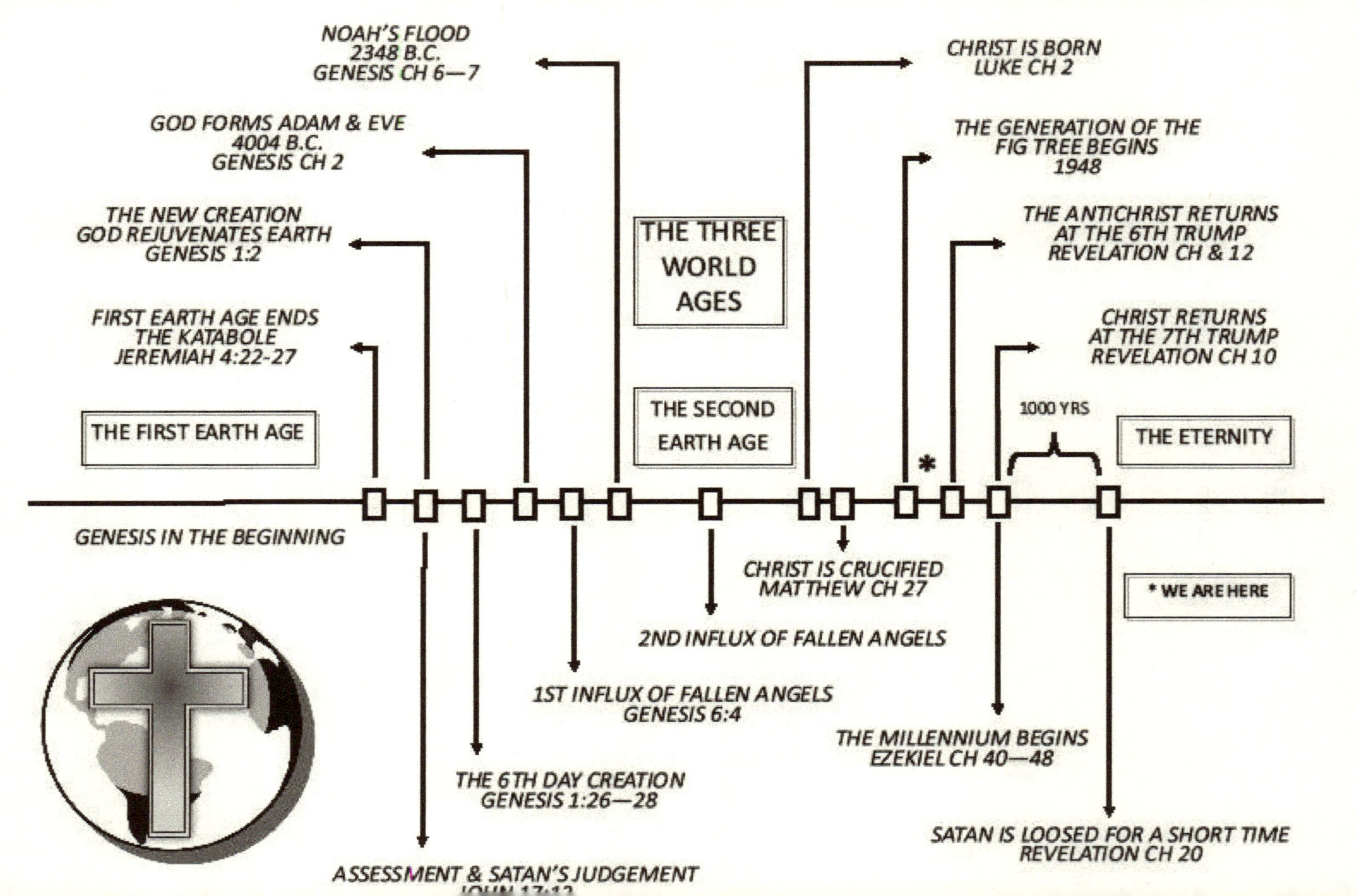

THE THREE WORLD AGES
THE FIRST EARTH AGE
THE SECOND EARTH AGE
THE ETERNITY
GENESIS IN THE BEGINNING
FIRST EARTH AGE ENDS THE KATABOLE JEREMIAH 4:22-27
ASSESSMENT & SATAN'S JUDGEMENT
THE NEW CREATION GOD REJUVENATES EARTH GENESIS 1:2
THE 6TH DAY CREATION GENESIS 1:26—28
GOD FORMS ADAM & EVE 4004 B.C. GENESIS CH 2
1ST INFLUX OF FALLEN ANGELS GENESIS 6:4
NOAH'S FLOOD 2348 B.C. GENESIS CH 6—7
2ND INFLUX OF FALLEN ANGELS
CHRIST IS BORN LUKE CH 2
CHRIST IS CRUCIFIED MATTHEW CH 27
THE GENERATION OF THE FIG TREE BEGINS 1948
*
THE ANTICHRIST RETURNS AT THE 6TH TRUMP REVELATION CH & 12
CHRIST RETURNS AT THE 7TH TRUMP REVELATION CH 10
THE MILLENNIUM BEGINS EZEKIEL CH 40—48
1000 YRS
SATAN IS LOOSED FOR A SHORT TIME REVELATION CH 20
* WE ARE HERE

SEQUENCE OF EVENTS IN THE END DAYS

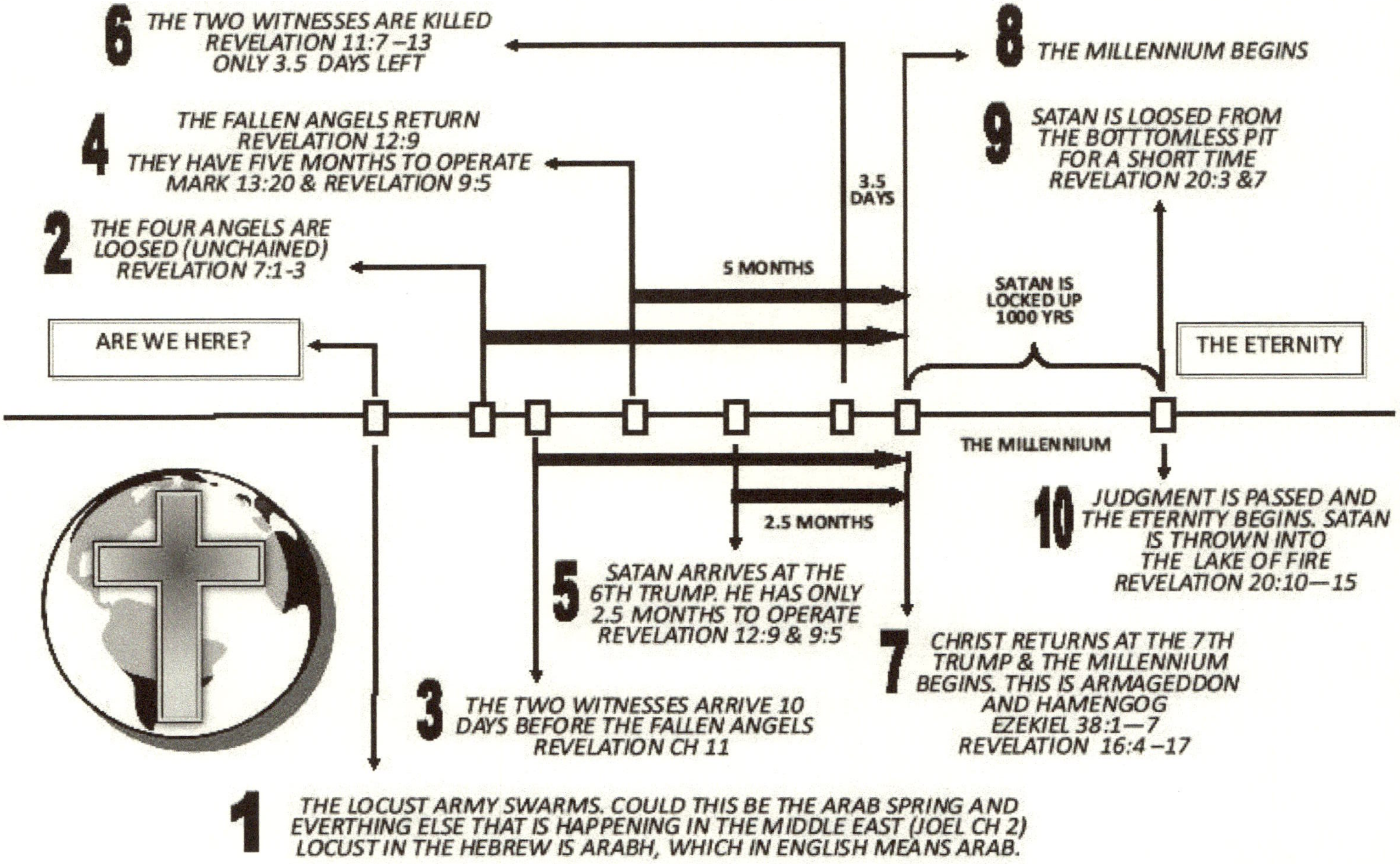

1 THE LOCUST ARMY SWARMS. COULD THIS BE THE ARAB SPRING AND EVERTHING ELSE THAT IS HAPPENING IN THE MIDDLE EAST (JOEL CH 2) LOCUST IN THE HEBREW IS ARABH, WHICH IN ENGLISH MEANS ARAB.

ARE WE HERE?

2 THE FOUR ANGELS ARE LOOSED (UNCHAINED) REVELATION 7:1-3

3 THE TWO WITNESSES ARRIVE 10 DAYS BEFORE THE FALLEN ANGELS REVELATION CH 11

4 THE FALLEN ANGELS RETURN REVELATION 12:9 THEY HAVE FIVE MONTHS TO OPERATE MARK 13:20 & REVELATION 9:5

5 MONTHS

5 SATAN ARRIVES AT THE 6TH TRUMP. HE HAS ONLY 2.5 MONTHS TO OPERATE REVELATION 12:9 & 9:5

2.5 MONTHS

6 THE TWO WITNESSES ARE KILLED REVELATION 11:7 –13 ONLY 3.5 DAYS LEFT

3.5 DAYS

7 CHRIST RETURNS AT THE 7TH TRUMP & THE MILLENNIUM BEGINS. THIS IS ARMAGEDDON AND HAMENGOG EZEKIEL 38:1—7 REVELATION 16:4 –17

8 THE MILLENNIUM BEGINS

SATAN IS LOCKED UP 1000 YRS

THE MILLENNIUM

9 SATAN IS LOOSED FROM THE BOTTTOMLESS PIT FOR A SHORT TIME REVELATION 20:3 &7

10 JUDGMENT IS PASSED AND THE ETERNITY BEGINS. SATAN IS THROWN INTO THE LAKE OF FIRE REVELATION 20:10—15

THE ETERNITY

CONTENTS

ACKNOWLEDGMENTS

Thanks to Dr. Arnold Murray for his lifetime of teaching and his gift of making the 'Word of God' understandable.

A special thanks to John C. May and Marci Lynn McGuinness. Their publishing, marketing and business skills made this book possible.

The quotes used in this book are solely for reference and are from the *Standard King James 1611* version *Bible*.

INTRODUCTION

You can't see it, but you can feel it...

"Something evil this way comes."

You can count on it. All the prophetic tumblers are falling into place – one after the other, faster and faster. The world is falling apart right before your very eyes and you cannot help but wonder what will happen next. Could this really be the end? You know enough to know that it will end, but not how or when. You tell yourself to relax and that everyone who has ever been born, at some point, believed that the world would end in his or her lifetime. The difference is that they were wrong, and you are right. We are living in the end times.

This earth age is at its end, and I will use God's words to prove it. It does not matter if you believe in God or not. He exists. How it ends is written, and it will happen exactly as it is written. You can count on it.

If you do believe in God, great – the biggest hurdle is jumped. If you do not, you will after you read this book.

Consider this: it is written that God came to this earth as flesh. He was to be called "Emmanuel," which interpreted means 'God with us'. His given name was Jesus Christ. For anyone who doubts the significance of the birth of this one man, know this – all time is recorded around the birth and death of this one man.

Before the birth of Jesus Christ, the widely accepted savior of men, time was recorded as B.C. or 'Before Christ.' After the death of this one man, all time and the means by which it was recorded changed. After his death, all time, whether in Canada or China, the United States or Russia, has been recorded as A.D. or Anno Domini. This means 'In the year of the Lord.'

Whether you believe in God or not, the end of this earth age is here, and it is going to happen. Don't you want to know how it comes down? It is my wish and the purpose of this book to explain just that. This is not a book on how to read the Bible, but when you finish it, you should be able to do just that.

The purpose of this book is to reveal the antichrist – who he is, how he arrives, with whom he comes and the events that will lead up to his coming. This revelation is a process that is necessary to fully understand his background, and he has quite a background. You will never guess who he is. However, he will be so convincing that the Bible states, "He will deceive the whole world." How could this possibly happen, especially at a time when no secrets exist? Having written the book, all I can say is to keep on reading, and you will not be disappointed.

Prepare yourself to read of things that you will never hear from the pulpit. Not because they are secrets, but because the preachers do not know.

We will travel through the Bible and uncover all there is to know about this evil entity and finally go further to expose this sinister fraud and reveal his diabolical plan to destroy your soul. The journey you are about to embark upon will be a life changing process in which its by-product will be your new ability to read and understand the Bible on your own.

Exposing and truly understanding who the antichrist is cannot, in my opinion, be done simply by telling someone. Grasping fully the magnitude of his beast system is far more complicated than that. Only by knowing how he came into being and the events that shaped him can a mortal man accept the truth. I hope by now I have peaked your interest enough to keep you reading this book. This is not a shell game or a bait and switch tactic. All the questions previously mentioned will be answered, plus many, many more.

I believe the journey you are about to embark upon as well as the knowledge you will be given will be well worth the effort, so much so that I am even willing to give away the ending of this book now at its beginning. I am comfortable doing this because there will be numerous times you will seriously doubt it is possible.

We win – that is how it ends. It is not the ending or even the process that would give the book away, but the twist at the end.

This twist is a curve ball in the greatest story ever told, the Bible. Believe me, you want to know how it ends. Your soul depends on it.

I am going to use verses directly from the Bible to document every statement I make. However, if I do give my opinion, I will say so. My opinion will be an educated guess based on my knowledge of the Bible.

I believe as you soon will, that we are in the end time. As the angel told Daniel in Chapter 12, verse 4,

"But thou, Daniel shut up the words and seal up the book, even to the time of the end. "And verse 10, "many shall be purified, and made white, and tried; but the wicked shall do wickedly: and none of the wicked shall understand; but the wise shall understand."

This prophesy was given to Daniel nearly 2500 years ago. This is your golden opportunity to take part in the fulfillment of prophesy.

CHAPTER 1

SOME BASICS TO READING THE BIBLE

The Bible is the best-selling book ever written. Year in and year out, it out-sells all other books. It is estimated that total sales surpass the 5 billion mark. That being said, it remains the most controversial and misunderstood book ever written.

There is a simple answer to this dilemma. That answer is that very few people truly know how to read the Bible with understanding. This would explain why so many Bible owners rarely open the book. It is a shame that it is most often used to store birth, marriage and death records, because this book has within its pages virtually all the answers to the questions that plague mortal man.

Some of these questions are:

- Why are we here?
- What really was the sin in the garden?
- How exactly does this age end?
- When?
- Is evolution true?
- Are there animals in heaven?
- Is global warming true or not?
- Do UFO's exist?

The answers to these questions and hundreds more are in the Bible.

Reading *A Time Has Come* is a journey, a journey throughout the ages, literally. A journey that starts at the very beginning of God's recorded time and ends in the near future. A journey that in its process will uncover and reveal the antichrist for exactly who and what he is. Only by understanding the ages can this be done accurately.

We will travel all the way back to the first earth age to discover just who the antichrist really is, and more importantly, his plan of deception. There is only one book that holds the answers to all the questions that will arise.

That being said, Our Father told us in Mark 13:23.

"Behold I have foretold you all things."

There really aren't any mysteries when you read the Bible verse by verse with a true understanding. That depth of understanding can only be obtained by knowing the keys first.

Whether you have read parts of the Bible or the entire text all the way through, I guarantee you do not know most of what is going to be revealed to you during your journey through this book.

Because I use the Bible as my primary basis for documentation, it is going to be important to establish its credibility, and we'll do just that. Never let anyone tell you that the Bible is full of contradictions. It's only those unlearned in Our Father's word who will make such a statement.

It has been said over and over that you can give the same verse from the Bible to ten different people and receive ten different interpretations of that verse. I agree. I can even tell you the reason this occurs. Most people when reading the Bible, do not apply the first rule of reading.

The Bible is the classic example of a book wherein you must pick up the subject and the object to rightly divide the message. I am going to use many verses as documentation while explaining their meaning, I will always apply these rules. The Bible is separated into chapters and verses. For the most part, each chapter has its own subject, which again for the most part, is established at the beginning of that chapter. However, there are more than a few exceptions, and you must stay aware of this. Some chapters have within them two or more subjects and therefore the object changes. I will give you a classic example of the importance of identifying the subject before this somewhat tutorial chapter is at its end. Again, this is not a book about learning how to read the Bible – that will happen as part of the process. I want to make you knowledgeable enough to be able to check my knowledge out for yourself. It is just that important.

I want to crush another all too common statement. This is the statement that the Old Testament does not apply today. This statement is not true. The Old and New Testaments are inseparably linked. One without the other would make understanding the Bible impossible. If you do not know what happened in the beginning, you will never understand how it is going to end. We are going to dispel the fairy tale about Eve and the apple. That will require the Old Testament. Christ himself quoted from the Old Testament on many occasions, and as you will discover, there is still prophesy from the Old Testament that has yet to be fulfilled. In addition, there is prophesy from the treasure chest of wisdom that is the Old Testament that is being fulfilled at this very time at a rapid pace.

I will be using the Old Testament and the New Testament as we move along together in our quest to expose the antichrist and his plan. Giving you the ability to read and interpret verses for yourself is of the utmost importance to me. This will allow you to discern the meaning that Our Father is trying to convey to the reader.

I invite and encourage you to follow along with any verse in your Bible, thereby checking me out for yourself through God's word. Also, it is absolutely fine with God to make notes in your Bible. It is your playbook for this life.

I made the statement that I have nothing to hide. Therefore, I will break down verses first, by identifying the subject and staying with that subject as it applies to any verses that follow. If you do not read within the subject, you will never know exactly what message Our Father wants us to take from his writings. There is a real danger in taking a verse and just running slipshod with it. When God sets the subject, no man has the right to change it. Why? Judgment begins at the pulpit, and that also goes for teachers.

Let's use a popular verse from the Bible as an example, Luke 12:48. Some people use this verse to put a guilt trip on those who have been blessed with success. Never apologize for being well off with the blessings of God. If you earned it honestly, you have every right to enjoy it. God owns everything, and he rewards those who love him and work hard. It is an insult to him when we do not appreciate his blessings. Luke 12:48 states partially.

"For unto whomsoever much is given, of him shall much be required. In other words, "To whom much is given much is expected".

I have heard preachers, pastors, priests and even a sitting President of the United States use this verse out of context (subject) in an attempt to guilt those who have been blessed by God with wealth (perceived wealth), to justify taking their money. You may think this lesson is a little off the antichrist topic, but it is perhaps not as far a stretch as you might think.

Just think about it. Using God's word out of context is flat out wrong and with so many of his children biblically ignorant, God hates this tactic with a passion. Why does God have such disdain for this kind of pandering? This tactic has caused far too many people to feel guilty, and in some cases even abandon their wealth. The problem here is twofold.

One, this statement is only part of the verse and is therefore misleading. Two, and almost criminal, is that the subject of this verse has nothing to do with money. The subject of this verse Luke 48 is set back in verse 37 of the chapter. The subject of this verse is "knowledge" in God's word, and nothing else. It is certainly not about money. Picking up and staying within the subject is imperative when reading the Bible. The bottom line is that it is all right to enjoy your blessings, but always give God the credit.

On that same subject, if God blesses you with knowledge, he expects you to share it, and you are now held to a higher accountability for the privilege of that knowledge. He doesn't hold someone who is a babe in His word to the same accountability as he does an adult in that same word. It makes perfect sense. It is fair.

It is not fair when a man who is supposed to be wise in God's word delivers a verse like this out of context to someone blessed with wealth (and I am not necessarily talking tremendous wealth). It is a tactic used to make them feel guilty, sometimes to the point that they give it away because they are told that they can't get to heaven if they have wealth. They have earned it. God blessed their efforts, and then a "man of the cloth" infuses guilt and they give it away.

Yes, I am well aware of the eye of a needle analogy, but that applies only to ill-gotten gains. How do you like it when someone returns your gift? God has feelings, too. After all, He is Our Father. I will explain and make real world, our relation with Our Father (God) in the next chapter. It is impossible to fully understand the origin of the relationship between you and Our Father (your Creator) without knowing that there was an age before this flesh age.

Let's spend a little time documenting the Bible's credibility. The Bible, all of it, contains God's words and thoughts that are only penned by man. Man simply records them as directed by God. Your documentation of this can be found in 2 Timothy 3:16.

"All scripture is given by inspiration of God and is profitable for truth, proof, guidance and righteousness.

Paul also gives credence in 1 Corinthians 10:11, talking about the Bible.

"Now all these things happened unto them for ensamples (examples)*: and they are written for our admonition* (warning), *upon whom the end of the world are come."* (That is us).

The bottom line is that the Bible is to be read, understood and trusted. After all, it is Our Father's way of communicating with his children during this, the second earth age. No matter who you are or the color of your skin, one common thread runs through all of us. We are all God's children. I know that sounds cliché, but it won't after reading the second chapter of this book. Another thing we all have in common is that there is a judgment coming, and God knows that accurate record keeping is essential to a fair trial.

"All men are (were) created equal." That is what our founding fathers wrote. Did they know something that 99.999 percent of the population today does not know? These words are true, however, we were not created in this earth age. We were born of woman, innocent, with no recollection of the first earth age. To prove if, we will follow God or satan. Keep in mind that there was an earth age before this one.

Let me be clear – the purpose of this book is as the cover states, to reveal the antichrist. To do this, the most basic knowledge in the Bible will be needed. I was raised Catholic and therefore had no knowledge of the Bible. There was a time when I could not navigate a Bible to save my soul. For example, my cousin and I were raised as close as any brothers. He is very intelligent and successful, yet he once asked me if the book of Deuteronomy was written by a guy named 'Dude.' In defense of Catholics, I was taught discipline and could tie a full Windsor knot at the age of seven. If you are someone blessed and are well learned in the Bible, be prepared to go to another level.

Let us begin our journey by answering this frequently asked question: What is the Bible? Simply put, the Bible is the story of one Man's family, Jesus Christ. Other nations and peoples are mentioned only inasmuch as they come into connection with Christ's genealogy. Christ's lineage begins with Adam and Eve. We are however, all God's children. I want to make the point that the Bible's account of history is accurate. The Bible's primary purpose is not to be a history book. However, it is historically accurate, thus adding to its validity, and that is the point. Christ's family genealogy is recorded and can be found in the book of the apostle Luke chapter 3, starting with verse 23 and ending with verse 38 below.

"...which was the son of Enos, which was the son of Seth."

Seth was the second son of Adam and was Eve's third. He was born after Cain murdered Abel. Abel was the son of Adam, who was the son of God. We know that Joseph was Christ's Father by law only, so we are really looking at in Luke chapter 3 is Mary's pedigree.

Nonetheless, Adam is the great, great, great..... Grandfather of Christ through Mother Eve, umbilical cord to umbilical cord, as is recorded for you. It is for this reason that Eve is called 'the Mother of all living' in Genesis 3:20. Here is another opportunity to lie waste to another myth that is taught and widely accepted. Some, out of ignorance, use this biblical statement as documentation that Adam and Eve were the first human beings to inhabit this earth in this earth age. However, that belief is not true and is easily refuted. We will do exactly that when we get to chapter three of this book.

I will say it again – I will prove, using the Bible, that Adam and Eve were not the first people to inhabit this earth. No, the first people were not aliens, either. They were humans. Eve was not the first woman, but she is the 'Mother of all living,' spiritually speaking. Eve is the mother of Christ, umbilical cord to umbilical cord. And, if you do not believe in Jesus Christ and his ability to forgive sin, you are spiritually dead. How can this be? If you do not believe in Jesus Christ and his power to forgive sins, then you do not stand a chance of making Eternity. This is just a fraction of the myths still being taught that will be debunked in this book.

I study from a Standard King James 1611 Bible. I do so because the King James holds closest to the original manuscripts which is important for my research. The fact that there are a few bad translations in the King James in no way diminishes the overall accuracy of this Bible. They are easily identified and corrected.

The King James was written in 1611 A.D., some 400 years ago. This was the Elizabethan era as well as the time of William Shakespeare, which undoubtedly explains the thees and thous that so many people struggle with. That was the language of that time period. Nonetheless, thank God for their effort, for who knows what would have happened to the word of God had they not preserved and made it available to the common man.

Some modern versions of the Bible are out there today that have wandered so far from the manuscripts that it would be impossible to teach the truth using them. Be careful.

This book is a real world study of God's word, the Bible. I intend to bring truth to the many myths attached to it because of the traditions of men. Traditions of men are bad. Why? For one, they are what has made reading the Bible so difficult to understand.

When you throw out the myths and bilge that man has injected into God's word, it truly is the greatest story ever told. It is riveting. We are obviously not going to read the entire Bible cover to cover, but we are going to purge out the traditions of men that Christ called Leaven (yeast), in the process of revealing the antichrist. Mark 7:13 tells us:

"That man's traditions make void (of no effect) the word of God."

God hates when man changes his words, whether with good intentions or with bad. These harmless myths are nothing short of lies. Lies hide the truth and put blinders on the reader. We do know that from truth comes knowledge and knowledge is wisdom. In the words of Sir Winston Churchill, "A lie gets halfway around the world before the truth puts on its pants." When it comes to the Bible and revealing the antichrist, the time has come to put on our spiritual pants and run down the lies that have stood for centuries, and we will, every single one of them. "Anti" in the Greek language means "instead of."

We are approaching the end of this earth age, and there could not be a better time to understand the Bible. It is like holding tomorrow's newspaper right in your hands.

Imagine being the only one in a crowd of thousands who truly understands the events and the order in which they will transpire to bring about the end of this earth age. You will know exactly where we are when people all around you are asking, "What is going on and how did this happen?"

I have mentioned that the Bible has been called 'the greatest story ever told,' and it is. As in many of the greatest stories, there is an unforeseen twist at the end; The Bible has a twist that is so epic it could very well be the difference between one making the Eternity or being blotted out forever.

If you read this book, you will be holding in your hands all of the answers to the test that is unfolding as we speak. God, Our Father, has stated that he loves all his children and does not want to lose even one of them. It is for this reason He tells us in Mark 13:20.

"Behold I have foretold you all things."

And so He has. Let now be the time that you finally read from the Bible with understanding and find out. It will most surely change your life.

Reading the Bible with understanding is like opening a feed sack, the kind that is sewn shut. If you start correctly, they just zip open and it flows freely. However, if you don't, it just doesn't work out.

The information in this book is intended to reveal the secrets that culminate in these end days and teach the reader the keys and fundamentals that will allow him or her to check me out and discover other so-called mysteries for themselves. After all, what a feeling it is to be able to read and understand a book that many say cannot be fully understood. Well, it can be done. Most of the confusion is due to the fact that it is impossible to 'build a house starting with the second floor,' without a good, solid foundation.

Many times in the Bible, Our Father will use agricultural metaphors as with the feed sack analogy. God loves agriculture and his hardworking farmers. What is common to both is that farming and farmers require a great deal of common sense, often called 'horse sense.' When reading the Bible, it is very important to use common sense. 1 Corinthians 14:33 tells us that God is not the author of confusion, so if something you are reading does not make sense, re-read it. If necessary, re-check the subject. You cannot speed read the Bible. Even Evelyn Wood would not recommend that. I sincerely believe that what you are about to read will make sense. There is scripture that makes me confident in this. The simple fact is this: those who love God are programmed to know the truth when they hear it, as documented in Proverbs 8:8, God speaking.

"All the words of my mouth are in righteousness; there is nothing forward or perverse in them, (Verse 9) they are all plain to him that understandeth, and right to them that find knowledge."

When you honestly study God's word, it will make sense, and God considers an honest try perfect. Something else to keep in mind is rightly dividing the word of truth. In other words, one must be able to determine the time (age) and place that each verse is in reference to. This knowledge is necessary if you are going to ever fully understand God's message through the Bible. This is why we will discuss in depth in Chapter two the key periods of time, the three world ages.

Again, a key that is useful when reading the Bible lies in identifying the object. The object is who or what the message being given is directed toward. Without question, all messages are for the reader's enlightenment. However, with some messages, it is important to know, using the subject, to whom the message is directed. For example, when prophesy is given in days, the reader must know that it applies only to the children of the light, those who love and follow God's word. Light equals truth in these cases. When prophesy is given in moons or months, it applies only to the children of darkness. Darkness equals satan's children or those who will do evil. When God gives a warning it usually is prefaced with the word "if," a small word with a huge meaning. If you're trying your best, God is not mad at you.

One last thought – when it comes to reading the Bible with

understanding, always look for the subtle things. They can very often mean a lot. I know of a good example of this. Let us turn to the book of John, Chapter 8, and examine verse 44. This is the New Testament. Christ is being questioned by the scribes and the Pharisees at the temple in Jerusalem, the very location that still exists today. These are the so-called scripture lawyers of that day. The Pharisees, Sadducees and their scribes were a form of government that kept control over the religious masses. Control, and the fact that they collected and funneled money to the Roman government, are the only reasons they were allowed to exist. However, they are rapidly developing a problem with Christ, as his message and popularity are making them look like the hypocrites they are. In Chapter 44 of John, these legalists are confronting Christ with questions concerning scripture and scripture law. As with most of their attempts to trip up Christ, they underestimate to whom they are speaking. Imagine the arrogance – trying to trip up God with scripture, his own words. This bantering has been going on for the last 43 verses, and Christ has had enough. He proceeds to tell these sad sack trouble-makers just who they are. This exchange has so much depth to it that we will dissect it later. For now, we are looking for subtleties. This is John 8:44, Christ is talking to the scribes and Pharisees.

"You are of your father the devil, and the lusts of your father you will do. He was a murderer from the beginning, and abode not in the truth, because there is no truth in him. When he speaketh a lie, he speaketh of his own: for he is a liar and the father of it."

Notice that father, and any reference to the devil (satan), is lowercase (not capitalized). Why? Because Christ is talking about the devil directly and realistically, not as though he were a myth or a puff of air. Satan does not deserve the respect of capital letters, as used in verse 42 when Jesus is speaking of God Our Father. It is important to notice that in verse 42, Jesus said to them, the scribes and Pharisees:

"If God were your Father, you would love Me: for I proceeded forth and came from God; neither came I Myself, but He sent Me."

The subtleties between an upper case letter versus a lower case letter may seem insignificant, but I can assure you it is important when reading the Bible. The devil (satan) does indeed have children on this earth at this time. I am not crazy. Just hear me out. They are called Kenites (the word is in the Bible), and they are the sons and daughters of Cain. Brace yourselves for this one: Cain is the son of the devil as a result of the real sin in the garden. Truth is truly stranger than fiction, and I will prove it. I told you we would make myths give way to the plain truth and use God's word and common sense to do it. No tricks are applied here, just common sense and intelligence. This book will change the way you look at everything, and that is the God's honest truth.

Something to keep in mind as you are reading this book. This is a journey as well as a process. This book is not a romance novel or a spy thriller. There is a great deal of information that is about to be passed on to you. Read at your own pace. Do not hesitate to stop occasionally to meditate and let some things settle. Also, because pretty much anyone you ask today feels something is brewing over the horizon, I make the suggestion that you keep this book handy, especially when things really start to ramp up. As they do you should be able to identify them. And always ask the Holy Spirit for understanding. Mark 13:29.

"So you in like manner, when you shall see these things come to pass, know that it (the end) is nigh, even at the doors."

God's speed on your journey to the truth.

Father, if it is your will, open eyes and ears. Enjoy.

CHAPTER 2

THE THREE EARTH AGES

Did you know that there was an earth age before this one? There was, and that is a fact. This knowledge is information very few people living on this earth today are aware of. There was an earth age before this earth age, and there is one yet to come, the Eternity. The fact that there was an earth age before this one makes sense and is supported by scientists and archaeologists alike. The physical evidence is overwhelming. Facts are stubborn things – they just do not go away. That is right, the Bible agrees that there was an earth age before this one. It has always the same earth, only the ages have changed. Just take a minute to ponder it. Now ask yourself why it makes sense. The answer to this question lies in God's word, Proverbs 8:8-9 below tells us,

"All the words of my mouth (the Bible) *are in righteousness; there is nothing forward or perverse in them."* (No lies).

Verse 9: *"They are all plain to him that understands (has understanding), and right to them that find knowledge."*

Our Father instructs us to seek knowledge. That knowledge manifests itself in understanding. With that thought in mind, let us turn to the book of Genesis. Genesis is the first book in the Bible and was written by Moses, as were the four books that follow, Exodus, Leviticus, Numbers and Deuteronomy. The word Genesis means 'the beginning.' Let's start with Genesis 1:1.

"In the beginning God created the heaven and the earth."

Period. Notice this verse does not say when the beginning was. The beginning of the world, mother earth, the terrafirma, was millions of years ago, way back in the first earth age. The Bible gives us plenty of verses for documentation, and we are going to uncover them. However, because God's word requires the reader to also use common sense, we will look at the physical facts that cannot be denied. In this chapter we are going to put the "link" in the missing link. Continuing in the book of Genesis verse 2.

"And the earth was without form and void; and darkness was upon the face of the deep."

There is glaring error in this verse. The original Hebrew manuscripts clearly state that the earth "became" void, not that the earth *"was void."* This error is easily corrected by using the Strong's Concordance of the Bible. The word "was" is #1961 in the Concordance. All five manuscripts from which the King James Bible was constructed state that "the earth became void. "If this verse were correctly written it would make teaching that there are in fact (3) world or if you will, earth ages, a lot easier. This is the missing link that takes the blinders off when reading the Bible. The Bible does not conflict with geology or archaeology. On the contrary it agrees that the earth, this earth, is millions and millions of years old. Proper translation of this one verse should go a long way to bringing evolutionists and creationists closer together. Having the knowledge that the earth became void we now need to explore "why" and "how" it became void. The how is easy – it was by God's hand. The answer to why is a longer story. We will search God's word in depth and answer that question. The short answer is that it happened because of pride and satan's rebellion in that age.

Most people of varying religions are aware of satan's rebellion, but no one seems to know where to place it in time. If they do, they are not talking or teaching it with the exception of a very few. Satan's rebellion took place at the end of the first earth age and is the reason God ended that age. I will back this statement up biblically. Let us travel back in time millions of years ago, to the first earth age.

Everything is perfect. The sun is shining, and the sky is a color of blue that is indescribable to we mere mortals in this flesh age. There is no pain, not even a thought of it. There is no stress or boredom, as we are in our spiritual, celestial, or eternal bodies, (all the same body however, they have several names). If at any time you have ever wondered why a loving, powerful and all-knowing God could not have created better bodies than these fragile, corruptible flesh bodies, the answer is that He did, in this first age. Our flesh bodies in this second earth age are all part of the arduous test that is this flesh age. They may seem like a punishment at times but God's plan is perfect. If you doubt this as I once did, you will not by the time you finish this book.

Let's return to the utopia that was the first earth age. All of God's children, us, go about our daily business working and playing among one another and with our animals. We are enjoying the world (this earth) that Our Father created and has chosen to share with us. We worked in the first earth age, documentation Isaiah 65:17-25, especially, verses 22 and 23. There were also cities in the first age (Jeremiah: 25-26). These verses will come up and be explained later in this chapter. However, there is nothing new under the sun (Ecclesiastes 1:9). God was pleased at that time, and why not? Pleasure, is the very reason he created us in the first place, documentation Revelation 4:11.

"Thou art worthy, O Lord, to receive glory and honor and power; for thou hast created all things and for thy pleasure they are and were created."

Things truly seem perfect in that age, but are they? There was one being in the world at that time who was working his way up the ladder. His name is Lucifer and he sometimes goes by his self-proclaimed name, the Bright Morning Star. We know him today as satan.

For millions of years, the Morning Stars (God's pet name for us, his children in the first earth age) and the sons of God (also us) sang, danced and shouted for joy (Job 38:7). Everything was perfect. However, there was big trouble just over the horizon. A devastating storm was brewing, and its name was el diablo, the devil, satan.

Okay, let us return to the first earth age and uncover a mystery God truly wants us to discover. We will learn what made God so angry that he destroyed that age and caused all souls to pass through this age in flesh. Let's try to understand what happened. All souls, us, God's children, are loving life and just living the dream. Satan, however, is becoming a rising star, gaining popularity among the other stars of heaven. And why not? God himself states that he created satan, the "full pattern" as described in Ezekiel 28:12.

"Thou sealest up the sum." = (toknith) in the Hebrew language.

This means that 'God broke the mold when he created satan, full of wisdom and perfect in beauty.' There you have it – satan is not ugly, and he does not have horns and a tail. What satan does have plenty of is pride. Pride will ultimately be his downfall, documentation Ezekiel 28:12,15&17.

Verse 12: "thou (satan) sealest up the sum, full of wisdom, and perfect in beauty.

Verse 15:*"Thou was perfect in thy ways from the day that thou was created, until iniquity* (perverted pride) *was found in thee."* and...

Verse 17: *"Thine heart was lifted up because of thy beauty, thou hast corrupted thy wisdom by reason of thy brightness."*

Time moves on, although meaningless in our eternal bodies, and satan has worked all the way up, in that age, to the guarding cherub in charge of protecting the mercy seat. That is Christ's / God's throne. Satan, because of his arrogant and insatiable pride, was not content with the privilege of just guarding God's throne, not for long anyway. Drunk on pride and the lust for power that goes with this proclivity, satan makes his age-ending move to take over Our Father's throne. Rather than guard God's throne, satan sits on the throne and boldly claims to be God, documentation Ezekiel 28:2.

"Thus sayith the Lord. Because thy heart was lifted up, and thou hast said, I am a God, I sit in the seat of God."

How is that for arrogance? This cataclysmic event is today known as the overthrow or satan's rebellion. In the manuscripts it is known as the 'katabole,' a word that very few people have ever heard, much less understand. Yet this one event ultimately caused God, Our Father, to destroy the first earth age.

As the first earth age winds down to its end, satan, having started this coupe, is gaining power. Full of pride and claiming to be God, satan gathers from the ranks, his 7,000 fallen angels. This full-pattern egotist then uses all his God-given powers, charm and unabashed ability to lie and successfully deceive one third of God's children, our brothers and sisters, in that age into turning their backs on God and following him. More problematic is that the other two thirds of God's children stood by and did nothing.

After all life was good. They had all they felt they needed, so they did not want to get involved. They did not love Our Father enough to even take a side. This no doubt explains why God states in Revelation 3:16:

"So then because thou art lukewarm, and neither cold or hot, I will spue thee out of my mouth."

"Spue," in the Greek language, is "emeo" It means 'to vomit.' God's use of language here lets us know what he thinks of non-committal fence sitters. Suddenly there is trouble in paradise. Satan and his following are raising hell, rebelling against God and all that is Holy, while the lukewarm fence sitters look on hoping to just get along. Meanwhile, God is watching and waiting for those who would stand up to this ungodly revolution. Those who do will be called the Elect in this earth age.

This looks eerily similar to what is going on in the world today. It is just my opinion, but I believe that these lukewarm fence sitters of the first earth age are the non-committal, Utopian seeking, and let's-all-just-get-along group in today's earth age. After all, there is nothing new under the sun.

God, always long suffering and patient, calls on his generals, the Archangels Michael and Gabriel, to seek volunteers to fight and put down this rebellion. With satan as general, the 7,000 fallen angels as his captains, and a full third of God's children, some 4 billion souls strong were looking to take possession of heaven and all the souls in it. Indeed, the odds look long for the good guys but (Ezekiel 18:4) tells us, God speaking.

"Behold, all souls are mine," and

Romans 8:31: *"What shall we then say to these things? If God be for us, who can be against us*?"

Thanks to God, the archangels, and the very few who answered the call to glory, satan and his army were subdued. The very few of God's children who answered the call, chose a side and fought against satan, are in this earth age called God's Elect. Because God's Elect chose a side and joined the fight against satan in the first earth age during his rebellion, God knows He can count on them to stand against satan at the end of this earth age. At the end of this earth age? That is right. Satan will, very soon, rear his deceitful head again in this earth age. He will be loosed from his prison in heaven (that dimension) and return to this earth as antichrist, claiming to be Jesus Christ. God will once again call on His Elect to save the day. It is for this reason he calls them, in this earth age, his Chosen, as stated in Ephesians 1:4.

"According as He (God) *hath chosen us, in Him* (God) *before the foundation of the world, that we should be holy and without*

blame before Him (God) *in love."*

The "foundation of the world" is always a reference to the first earth age. Another example is in Isaiah 43:10.

"You are My witnesses, saith the Lord, and My servant whom I have chosen."

Because they stood against satan in the first earth age, God also calls them His Elect. (The majority of the Elect are here on Earth at this time).

Isaiah 42:1. *"Behold My servant, whom I uphold; Mine Elect, in whom My soul delighteth."*

In 2 Peter 1:10, this verse covers both called and Elect.

"Brethren, give diligence to make your calling and election sure."

This is why being a preacher, priest or teacher does not necessarily mean you are called or one of the Elect. Knowing the truth in God's word, the truth we are discovering, is an absolute prerequisite. The other is compassion. Show me someone without compassion, and I will show you someone who is not an Elect – by assessment, not judgment. Remember, the Elect were chosen based on their action in the first earth age. God does not play favorites. Our Father's word makes direct reference to the Elect seventeen times in the Bible and his chosen many more times. These are the true and few heroes of satan's rebellion in the first earth age. Although there has always been a remnant of the Elect throughout this earth age, God will use the majority of them to give a testimony at the end of this earth age. That is when satan and the fallen angels return to this earth and once again try to capture the souls of God's children. How satan intends to pull this off is the greatest twist in the greatest story ever told, the Bible. To see how it ends, keep on reading.

There are other words referencing the Elect in the Bible, that without knowledge of the first earth age are impossible to correctly explain. Words like "predestinate" and "did foreknow," for example. Paul, in Romans 8:29 writes.

"For whom He (God) *did foreknow."* He also used predestinate in Romans 8:30, below.

"Moreover whom He did predestinate, them He also called: and when He called them He also justified: and whom He justified, them He also glorified."

Let's go ahead and break this verse down. "He (God) did foreknow." From when? Not from the womb as some teach. From the first earth age. This is why God could say in Jeremiah 1:5 that he knew Jeremiah before Jeremiah was even in his mother's womb:

"Before I formed thee in the belly I knew thee; and before thou camest out of the womb I sanctified (set apart) *thee and I ordained* (appointed) *thee a prophet unto all nations."*

God did this because of Jeremiah's actions in the first earth age. There can be no other explanation. Jeremiah earned the right to be one of God's prophets in this flesh age. The truth always makes sense to those who love God (Proverbs 8-9).

"Did predestinate" means chosen from the first earth age. God's Elect have a "destiny" to fulfill. *"He also called."* The Elect did not volunteer in this earth age. God drafted (chose) them because of their actions in the first earth age. He knows he can rely on them to carry out their assigned mission in this earth age. *"He also justified."* Justified means judged. God's Elect have already been judged. This judgment took place just after satan's rebellion of the first earth was crushed. The Elect, because of their actions before and during the rebellion, were found blameless. God then

determined that every soul he created in the first earth age must pass through this age in flesh, to make a choice. Will they follow God or satan. In other words, will those who followed satan in the first age choose God in this age. John 3:16 states that they only need to accept Jesus Christ to be back in God's family. And, will the fence sitters of that first earth age step up to the plate and choose God over satan? That is what this second earth age is about and how I justify the statement "God put us in flesh bodies as a chastisement and a test." The Elect did not deserve chastisement. They are here to help the others.

Here is a twist. Satan and the fallen angels, in an ultimate act of defiance, chose not to take on a flesh body at all. They instead would leave their place of habitation (that dimension) and come to this earth to seduce flesh women. Your documentation is in the Book of Jude. This topic will be covered in depth in the next chapter. For now, let it suffice to say that because of their decision, satan and his angels have already been judged and are sentenced to death. The fallen angel's sentences are to be carried out at the end of this earth age. Satan's sentencing will not happen until after the millennium. Both however will be destroyed in the Lake of Fire.

The Elect are saved, and satan and his angels are doomed. So what about the majority of the two thirds who didn't do anything at all? This is where God had a terrible choice to make, and I believe this caused our flesh age to come into being. I believe God could have destroyed the devil and his angels. This belief is supported by the fact that they are to this day sentenced to be destroyed. As far as the one third who turned their backs on God and followed satan, I feel that although it may have all but killed Him, Our Father probably would have been able to destroy them as well. It would not have been easy, however. Imagine what it would be like having to kill even one of your children, much less billions. God loves all his children very much as He tells us in 2 Peter 3:9.

"The Lord is not slack concerning His promise, as some men

count slackness; but is long suffering toward us, not willing that any should perish, but that all should come to repentance." (Choose to love him).

Considering all this, there was still the majority of the two thirds who did not care enough and did not love God enough to take a side. What was God to do with these cowards? This is where I believe God was faced with the toughest decision. How would he ever be able to trust these double-minded fence sitters for an Eternity? I know what you are thinking. God knows what we are thinking, so why can't he read their minds and find out?

Now comes the wild card in all of creation. Man has free will. I have documented that God created all souls (mankind) for His pleasure. That being said, God did not want a bunch of mind-numbed robots forced to love him. He, like us, wants true love. Agape love. When it comes to mankind, anywhere freedom of choice exists, ultimately, bad choices are made. Indecision was a bad choice. Based on God's obvious disdain for lukewarm souls, I feel He had no choice but to formulate a plan (test) for their salvation, a plan that would truly separate the chaff from the wheat. That plan? God would gather all souls back to Him and withdraw his light, thus destroying that age and leaving the earth covered with ice from pole to pole, 'void' or 'toha va bohu' in the Hebrew language. It is for this reason the manuscripts say in Genesis 1:2 that the earth became void. God does not create anything void. He created the earth to be inhabited in this age and before, in the first earth age, documentation Isaiah 45:18.

"For thus saith the Lord that created the heavens; God himself that formed the earth and made it; He hath established it, He created not in vain, He formed it to be inhabited: I am the Lord and there is no one else."

There you have it. God did it. How can someone call him or herself a Christian and believe in evolution? It just will not fly. God would, however, leave some remnants of the first earth age, perhaps as clues, or perhaps to substantiate his word to his children who love him enough to mindfully search that word in the form of fossils. Either way, God created the earth! This age, the one that was and the one to come, the Eternity. You should read it for yourself in 2 Peter chapter 3 verses 6&7.

As advertised, now is a good time to look at some physical evidence. There is a place in Nebraska called Ash Fall National Park. A location with many attractions, Ash Fall has one feature that truly stands out. Nestled in rural northeastern Nebraska, this park holds some of the best evidence of days long gone by. Tucked in a section of this park, archaeologists have unearthed the perfectly preserved remains of animals carbon dated to 50,000 plus years old. The remains of these animals are blanketed in several feet of white powdery volcanic ash, believed to be the result of an eruption of Mount St. Helen, many thousands of years ago. These fossils are intriguing enough at face value, however, the fact that all these animals are indigenous to the continent of Africa boggles the mind. Bones of zebras, lions, rhinoceros, elephants and others, wholly intact, raise the question, Why are they here in the United States? The most commonly held answer does not conflict with the Bible's explanation. If you take the east coast of the United States and match it with the western coast of Africa, you can see that it is a pretty good fit. Taking into consideration thousands of years of erosion, it is a very good fit. The answer is that at one time, back in the first earth age, these continents were together. God split them along with others, at the beginning of this earth age some 13,000 years ago.

It is no coincidence that He split the earth into seven continents, as well as seven seas. The number seven in biblical numbers means 'spiritual completeness and perfection.' Numbers have significance in God's world.

Physical clues allow us license to speculate that in the first earth age the earth was one land mass, lush, green and inhabitable everywhere, as will be documented. In light of the fact that our eternal bodies have no use for water (H20) as we know water today, the firmament (the Bibles description of water H20) was above the earth, surrounding it and protecting it like a transparent, viscous cocoon, filtering away any would-be harmful solar effects. With the protection of the firmament above, there was no jet stream, therefore the weather and climate were perfect. Evidence supporting the belief the earth was one land mass, lush, green and inhabitable all over its surface is demonstrated in archaeology. Archaeologists have found the remains of mastodons (dinosaurs) in the Arctic Circle with a buttercup flower preserved in its enormous mouth. This is not an isolated case. Based on this immutable find, one can only arrive at two conclusions. Flowers do not grow in the arctic region today so this must be the first earth age, and there were dinosaurs in that age. The Bible documents this in Job 40:15-17. In verse 15, God calls this dinosaur a 'behemoth, a grass eater' and compares its tail to that of a Cedar tree. This is undoubtedly in reference to a Lebanon Cedar. These trees were strong, straight, and tall, so much so that they were used to make masts to support the sails of great ships. More evidence of a perfect earth has been discovered in Arizona. At very high elevations, above the tree line, fossilized Palm trees have been unearthed. The Bible speaks of creation while man speaks of evolution. Every evolutionist's theory has in it a hole of one sort or another. For evolution to be a viable explanation, it would have to still be going on today, would it not? Where is the evidence? I defy you to show me the amoeba, that is today's chicken, then show me every stage of the development in between. It cannot be done. It is just not possible, and neither is the evolution theory. It is not my intention to offend anyone. However your soul depends on your knowledge of the truth.

Apply the evolution theory to flesh man, and it becomes even more ridiculous. Man can adapt (cold, hot, etc.), but he is basically the same as he was when God created him several thousand years ago in this earth age.

Contained within the borders of a private park in New Mexico sits a large rock. Nearly centered on the surface of this rock is a human footprint. There are, upon this enormous boulder, several other less pronounced prints, but this footprint is clearly defined.

It is a size eight with a perfect instep, identical to that of a human's footprint today. Experts believe the being that made it tripped, planting that foot heavily in the sediment in an attempt to catch his balance. The footprint carbon dates to more than 50,000 years old. This print is identical to the foot of a man with a size eight foot today. I will document, using God's word that angelic beings' bodies do have mass. Let's start with Genesis 1:1.

"In the beginning God created the heaven and the earth," all the way to Revelation 10:6.

"And swear by Him (God) *that liveth forever and ever, who created heaven, and the things that therein are, and the earth, and the things that therein are, and the sea that therein are, that there should be time no more."*

As well as 43 times in between, God's word states that he created everything. There is simply no room for evolution. Having your eyes opened to the fact that there was a first earth age is the foundation to fully understanding the Bible.

God's plan for salvation is said to be perfect, and it is. However, in order for His plan to be perfect He knew He would need to have a safety net built in to gather together those who may never have had a chance to hear the real truth in His word, during this earth age. That is the very truth you are reading right now. In order to accomplish this, He would create the millennium. The millennium, by definition, would be a period of time, 1,000 years, wherein those who did not get a chance to hear the truth in this earth age as well as those who for one reason or another failed this test, could be taught that truth. There would of course have to be some penalty involved for not seeking out this truth, especially, for those alive on the earth in the end days when the antichrist appears. With the decision made, that penalty is as follows: Those who do not overcome in this second earth age, the flesh age, will, rather than be with Christ, have to remain away from His loving presence for the 1000 years of the millennium. This is reason enough alone to learn that truth.

Let's return once again to the first earth age. It is the end of the katabole, which is the biblical name for satan's rebellion. Everything has calmed down and God's mind is made up as to how things are to move forward. He does, however, take a moment to reflect. Looking at the earth, God assesses the damage that was the first earth age. What God sees and his thoughts are recorded in the book of Jeremiah. Let's visit Jeremiah 4:19-31 now.

Verse 19: "*My bowls, my bowls!* (Bowls means gut – the entire scenario pained God at his very core). *I am pained at my very heart; my heart maketh a noise in me; I cannot hold my peace, because thou hast heard, o my soul, the sound of the trumpet, the alarm of war.*"

God did not take any pleasure in what satan forced Him to do. It broke His heart. The trumpet spoken of in this verse is the same trumpet that will sound at the seventh trumpet in this earth age announcing Christ's returns.

Verse 20: "*Destruction upon destruction is cried; for the whole land (earth) is spoiled: suddenly are my tents spoiled, and my curtains in a moment.*"

In a moment in the Hebrew language is 'rega,' which means 'in a blink of an eye.' How long the actual rebellion lasted is not known, but when God had enough, it was over in the blink of an eye. He will use the same swiftness at the end of this earth age (1 Corinthians 15:52) documents it. Back to Jeremiah Ch. 4.

Verse 22: "*For my people is foolish, they have not known me; they are sottish children, and they have none understanding: they are wise to do evil, but to do good they have no knowledge.*"

The very same situation is going on right now in this earth age. People simply do not take the time to know God. How do you do this? By reading the letter He wrote to us, the Bible, which is Our Father's way of communicating with us in this flesh age. God has seen to it that the Bible contains all the information that is necessary for His children to gain the Eternity. By the way, "sottish" means 'stupid.' verse 23, God speaking.

"I beheld the earth, and lo (look), *it was without form and void, and the heavens, they had no light."*

This verse describes what God sees as He looks at the earth, or what is left of it, mere moments after he had destroyed the first earth age. Notice the words 'void' and 'without form.' These are the same words used in Genesis 1:2. We know by this verse we are somewhere between the first earth age and the second earth age. This documents the use of the words 'became void,' when speaking of Genesis 1:2. The earth was not created void. God destroyed that age. Once again it is impossible to fully understand the Bible without knowing this fact.

This event is the foundation to fully understanding the Bible. How long the earth sat void while we, God's children, remained with Him in heaven is not expressly written. It is believed by some, myself included, that the time between ages was 25,800 years. This theory is based on a galactic alignment of the stars. On December 21, 2012, the planets and certain stars aligned in a way not seen in 25,800 years. This is a bit more than a theory and for what it's worth, the fact remains that the earth, by God's hand, did become void for a lengthy period of time, Jeremiah verse 24.

"I beheld the mountains, and lo, they trembled, and all the hills moved lightly."

God looks, as the earth is still reeling from the blow. The force of the firmament (the suspended water surrounding the earth) crashing down, has the earth shaking and without the sun's warmth, it quickly becomes a ball of formless ice, verse 25.

"I beheld, and lo, there was no man, and all the birds of the heavens were fled."

This verse is yet more documentation that there was a first earth age. This is the reason it is so very important to carefully identify time frames or, better said, periods of time. Do not just read over that there was no man and all the birds were gone. This is quite clearly not the flood of Noah's time. There were plenty of birds as well as animals when Noah opened the door to the ark. The flood of Noah's time would not take place until 2,348 B.C. In this, the second earth age, here is another fact: Noah's flood only lasted one year. Your documentation is in Genesis 7:6.

"And Noah was six hundred years old when the flood of the waters was upon the earth." And the floods end, Genesis 8:13.

"And it came to pass in the six hundredth and first year, (of Noah's life) *in the first month, the first day of the month, the waters were dried up from the earth."*

Noah removed the covering of the ark and looked, and behold, the face of the earth was dry. Bottom line: Noah's flood did not destroy the earth, leaving it void. The earth was immediately habitable, and the ark contained two of every flesh that you see today, only a short 4,000 and some years later. That is not much time for evolution to do its thing, verse 26 Jeremiah.

"And I beheld, and lo, the fruitful place was a wilderness, and all the cities thereof were broken down at the presence of the Lord and by his fierce anger."

Do not read over this verse, either. It not only describes total destruction, but it tells us of some other observations on God's part that are very interesting. 'All the cities' is documentation that there were in fact cities in the first earth age. I bet you didn't know that. The fact that there were cities makes sense. It will be documented in the next chapter, our spiritual or celestial or angelic or heavenly, or immortal or eternal bodies, (all the same body) have mass. They are not puffs of air. It therefore makes sense that they need a dwelling, not unlike our flesh bodies. Ecclesiastes 1:9 tells us that,

"The thing that hath been, it is that which shall be; and that which is done is that which shall be done: and there is no new thing under the sun." Never has been and never will be.

Isaiah 65:17. This verse sets the subject and the time frame which is the Eternity.

"For behold I create new heavens and a new earth: and the former shall not be remembered, nor come to mind."

I am sure you have heard this at some time or another, but now you have it right in front of you in Our Father's own words. We will not remember this earth age any more than we remember the first one now. There may be an occasional de-ja-vu like most of us have experienced in this age, but that is just my opinion. The above verse documents that we are in the Eternity. After all, the prophet Isaiah lived in this flesh age. He prophesied from 649 BC to 588 BC, a short 2600 years ago. Staying in the book of Isaiah and Chapter 65, let's skip down to verse 21 and that we will once again have houses in the Eternity.

"And they (us) *shall build houses, and inhabit them; and they shall plant vineyards and eat the fruit, of them.*

Verse 22. *"They shall not build, and another inhabit; they shall not plant and another eat."*

What God is telling us here through Isaiah, is that there will be no usury in the Eternity, as in no borrowing with interest. We build it. We own it, although I am sure there will be group participation.

The point is that everything belongs to God now and in the Eternity. Our Father chooses to share it with his children in that age. Anyone who claims to own what belongs to God and uses it to exploit his (God's) children will simply not have a job in the Eternity, if they make it. Continuing with verse 22 of Isaiah.

"For the days of a tree are the days of my people."

This is referring to an oak tree. Man may live to be one hundred years old, but an oak tree to hundreds of years. If a man is born in flesh and at the same time an oak tree is planted, the man will never live long enough to see the death of the oak tree. This is a Hebraism for eternal life, verse 23.

"They shall not labor in vain."

Yes, we will work in the Eternity, but as the adage states: if you do what you love, you will never work a day in your life. Our work in the Eternity will truly be a labor of love, verse 24.

"And it shall come to pass, that before they (God's children) call, I will answer; and while they are yet speaking, I will hear them."

What God is saying to the wise here is, in the Eternity, there will be no anxiety. He knows our needs and will meet them even before we ask, verse 25.

"And the lion shall eat straw like the bullock."

This answers the question, will there be animals in heaven?

There is no flesh in heaven, thus no carnivores (flesh eaters) even the wildest beast will be tame. Let us return to the book of Jeremiah, Chapter 4, and pick back up with verse 27. We are once again between the first and second earth ages, verse 27 reads,

"For thus hath the Lord said, the whole land (earth) shall be desolate; yet will I not make a full end."

Remember, God has just destroyed the first earth age. He is angry and it is understandable. The rebellion that had just taken place is nearly impossible to comprehend. One of God's most trusted and loved (satan), along with the fallen angels, successfully persuaded one third of God's children to turn against him. God, rather than destroy any of his children, has formulated a plan. He would require every soul ever created in the first earth age to pass through this age in flesh. Each soul would be born of woman innocent (this fact discredits the doctrine of original sin as is held by some), with no recollection of that first age, to make the choice whether they will ultimately follow God or satan.

Let's look at baptism and some documentation that disproves the man held tradition that is "original sin." I want to be clear, I believe in baptism. However, what is baptism really? Baptism is an affirmation of your faith. To be done correctly, without shortcuts, the one being baptized should be totally submersed in water symbolizing your belief that Christ died, was placed in the tomb and rose from that tomb three and a half days later. This act has to be made by someone mature enough to make that decision and certainly an infant cannot. Neither can a young child for that matter. Their slate is clean. No one born in flesh is responsible for the sins of their parents, including the sins of Adam and Eve. Everyone has their own ship to sail in this age, and besides, there were plenty of people running around on this earth no doubt sinning before Adam and Eve came along. There was no original sin. Jeremiah 31:29-30 tells us, "In those days they shall say no more, the fathers have eaten a sour grape, and the children's teeth are set on edge." Verse 30,

"But everyone shall die for their own iniquities (sins): every man that eateth a sour grape, his teeth shall be set on edge."

Simply stated: everyone will answer for their own sins. There will be no finger pointing on Judgement Day. I wanted to make this point for anyone that has lost a child that was not baptized. You may rest assured that child is at home and with the Lord (in that dimension). I believe some are just too good to suffer this flesh experience. It is truly a shame that men dream up traditions that serve only to keep their sheep feeling guilty.

In looking back, we had it easy in the first age. Why? In our spiritual bodies, we had no flesh nagging at us, always whining and wanting. I am hungry, I am thirsty, I want, I want. That is the flesh condition. God knew this would be the case. I firmly believe that one of the reasons God put us through this flesh age is so we like Him, could feel what it is like to be a parent. If you stop to think about it, it makes sense. It is the only way that we, as his children, could have the shoe on the other foot, so to speak.

It is a sure bet that there is no gender in our eternal bodies. One reason is that in those bodies, we are always called sons of God and there is no giving and taking (procreation) in those eternal bodies. Check it out for yourselves. Documentation Luke 20:34-36.

"No matter what body we are in we are all Our Father's children, therefore no matter what body we may be in we are all siblings."

In this world, God wants us to learn to take care of one another. From caring for an infant and all that implies to holding someone's hand as they pass from this flesh age to Paradise. These are only feelings that can be obtained in the flesh experience. This is also why it is so important to know what satan's plan of deceit is and to share it with as many of your siblings as possible.

Let us go over it again, because it is just too important. The devil intends to deceive as many souls as he possibly can throughout this earth age. Satan, in his arrogance, believes that if he can claim victory over enough souls, God will have to back down, thus saving his (satan's) own soul.

Six billion plus souls have come and passed in this flesh age. There are some six billion plus souls on the earth at this time. All signs indicate that time is up. Satan believes his plan of deception will avert his own doom. You must be aware of how his plan unfolds in order to protect your soul.

Satan and the fallen angels, because of their actions in the first earth age and their decision not to be born in a flesh body, are doomed to the Lake of Fire. God, before he destroys them, will use these disobedient pawns to test every soul born in flesh and judge if they have passed the test. God has spoken it. It is written, therefore it shall come to pass, as is evident in Jeremiah 4:28.

"For this shall the earth mourn, and the heavens above be black: because I have spoken it, I have proposed it and I will not repent, (change my mind) *neither will I turn back from it."*

The blackness of space in this age appears to be void and lifeless. However, in the Eternity it will be alive, vivacious and bustling with activity, a universe full of life. We mortals have only to suffer this flesh age to experience it. Come Lord quickly.

The information in this chapter should answer the questions.

Why are we here on this earth at this time? And what is expected of us?

Furthermore, we now know why satan is our mortal enemy and that he was not created evil but became evil because of free will. It was his choice! With the exception of the Elect, whom with God reserves the right to intervene in their lives, everyone has their own ship to sail through this flesh age. "Free will." There will be no finger pointing on Judgment Day. Always keep this thought in mind. Our Father loves us and is pulling for us. He is there whenever we ask for help.

This is pretty much all there can be known about the first earth age. Having this missing puzzle piece, you now know what 99% of Christians do not know, "there was an age before this one." Having gained this wisdom, let us read about the beginning of this, the second earth age. You now read it with the blinders off. You simply will not believe what really took place in the Garden of Eden that fateful day.

CHAPTER 3

GENESIS: THE BEGINNING

Genesis 1:1: *"In the beginning God created the heaven and the earth."*

Period. It does not say when. Notice that heaven and earth are singular. This is the first heaven and the first earth. We have covered this in the last chapter, but let's look in God's word for additional documentation that there was in fact an age before this one. Let's look at 2 Peter 3:5. It will be helpful to keep your "three world graph" handy as we move through this chapter.

"For this they are willingly ignorant of, that by the word of God the heavens were of old (number one)*, and the earth standing out of the water, and in the water."*

2 Peter 3:6 is speaking of the first earth age just after the katabole' or 'satan's rebellion.'

"Whereby the world that was (number one) *being overflowed with water, perished."*

Again, the following verse is describing the destruction of the first earth age that we covered in the first chapter. God brought the firmament surrounding the earth crashing down and flooding the earth, as 2 Peter 3:7 describes.

"But the heavens and the earth which are now (number two, this age)*, by the same word are kept in store, reserved unto fire against the Day of Judgment and perdition of ungodly men."*

It is well documented and inarguable that there is an Eternity. The Eternity is earth age number three.

The above verse says a lot, so let's break it down. 'Reserved unto Fire' tells us how God will destroy this, the second earth age. He promised in the book of Genesis 9:11-13 that He would never again destroy an earth age by water. Then giving us the rainbow as the sign of His promise. He will destroy this age by fire. Furthermore, Hebrews 12:29 states *'For God is a consuming fire.'*

No worries – this fire is but a warming glow to those who love God. However, to those who are against Him, it is an all-consuming and destroying fire. Back to 2 Peter 3:8.

"But beloved be not ignorant of this one thing, that one day is to the Lord is as a thousand years (to man)*, and a thousand years as one day."*

Judgment day is often referred to in the Bible as 'The Lord's Day.' When God's word talks of the Lord's Day and Judgment Day (they are the same event), it is referring to the millennium, which by definition is a thousand years. One day to Our Father is a thousand years to mankind, and the millennium is a time of teaching for mankind. However, it is only one day to Our Father. We will describe the millennium in depth later, as the millennium is not considered an age but a period of time.

Another place in Our Father's word that documents that God does not create anything void, and that He created this earth to be inhabited, is Isaiah 45:18-19:

"For thus saith the Lord that created the heavens; God Himself, that formed the earth and made it; He hath established it, He created it not in vain (void, in the Hebrew, tohu va bohu). I am the Lord; and there is none else."

God formed the earth to be inhabited, this time, before, and in the Eternity. God does not create anything for nothing. Everything He does has a purpose, as we can see in Genesis 1:2.

"And the earth was (became) without form, and void: And the darkness was upon the deep. And the spirit moved upon the face of the waters."

And is a polysydenton in the Hebrew language. It means 'a lot more is happening than is being written'. You will see this often throughout Genesis and other books of the Bible as well. The time frame we are in is the very beginning of this earth age and things are moving right along. Remember, all five manuscripts, the writings from which the *King James Bible* was constructed, say the earth BECAME void. Was = became. This is a good time to expand on the events that took place immediately after satan's rebellion. We know God destroyed the previous age, the first earth age, because of satan's rebellion. The earth sat void for a long period of time. This is the gap on your graph, between the first world age and the beginning of this one. While the earth sat void all souls, God's children, us, are with him in heaven. Remember, the definition of heaven is "wherever God is." During that period of time, satan is tried, found guilty, and sentenced to death. How will this happen? The answer can be found in the Book of Ezekiel 28:17-18. Ezekiel means 'God strengthens.' The message in this verse was given to Ezekiel thousands of years ago and is yet future. The time of the fulfillment of this prophesy is at the very end of this earth age, during satan's tribulation, which is not long from now, in my opinion. Verse 17 states why satan is doomed and verse 18 describes what God is going to do to him as a result of his crimes.

"Thine (satan's) heart was lifted up because of thy beauty, thou hast corrupted thy wisdom by way of thy brightness: I will cast thee to the ground (earth), I will lay thee before kings, that they may behold thee."

Verse 18 "Thou hast defiled thy sanctuaries by the multitude of thy iniquities, by the iniquity of thy traffic; this is why we came here, *"therefore, I will bring forth a fire from the midst of thee, it shall devour thee, and I will bring thee to ashes upon the earth in the sight of all them that behold thee."* We are going to see it.

God is talking to satan here. He is going to turn him to ashes from within. Satan is doomed, thus he is called the 'Son of Perdition.' Perdition means 'dead,' however, Satan's sentence will not be carried out until the end of the millennium. Why wait? Satan has work to do. He is the negative part of God's plan in this world age. God is always fair. Every soul created in the first world age must pass through this world age in flesh to be tested, to prove that they truly love God and can be trusted in the Eternity. God and the Holy Spirit are the positive part of the plan. Every positive needs a negative, and this is satan's role. At this time, satan is here in spirit only, but as we see from Ezekiel 28:13, he has walked this earth in this age.

"Thou hast been in the garden of God."

Satan was in the Garden of Eden (God), in this earth age, as will be documented later in this chapter. Job 1:6-7 states that satan and the fallen angels have walked the earth in this earth age. The time is about 1706 B.C. We can see this clearly in verse 6, followed by verse 7:

"Now there was a day when the sons of God (these are the fallen angels) came to present themselves before the Lord, and satan came also among them."

"And the Lord said unto satan, whence comest thou? Then satan answered the Lord, and said, from going two and fro on the earth, and from walking up and down it."

Yes, satan and the fallen angels have been allowed to walk the earth in this earth age. They escaped from heaven as recorded by Jude 1. Jude was the brother of Jesus Christ and thus credible. They were not in flesh, however, satan and the fallen angels have never been or ever will be in a flesh body. The fallen angels are still in their celestial, angelic or eternal bodies. They, like satan, refused to take on a flesh body. It is for this reason they also are sentenced to death. If you want an in-depth account of their reasons for refusing flesh bodies like the rest of us, and their evil intentions in the not-too-distant future, keep reading.

This situation is problematic, as it means they are still supernatural, which simply means more natural, but, as we will discover a huge problem, nonetheless. Satan and his lieutenants will never be born of woman, innocent, with no knowledge of what happened in the first world age. They will have total knowledge. They may even know you or me. If you are one of God's Elect you can pretty well count on it. This makes them a powerful threat to us as well as to God's plan of salvation. The fallen angels have come and gone from time to time during this second earth age, but satan's time of imprisonment is specific. Christ, at the end of His 40-day temptation by satan, commands the devil in Luke 4:8 to.

"Get thee behind Me."

Satan at this time, and for the time being, is locked in chains in heaven by Michael, the Archangel. It is not until the sixth trumpet sounds that he and his fallen angels, at God's command, are cast to this earth. Thus begins the tribulation of this, the second earth age. Let's document this event in Our Father's word in the Book of Revelation 12:7-9. Chapter 12 of Revelation covers more time than pretty much any other book of the Bible. It starts in the first earth age and continues throughout satan's tribulation. Verse four of this chapter is where I document that a third of God's children followed satan in the first earth age. The book of Revelation is future therefore the events you are about to read of have not happened yet.

"And there was war in heaven: Michael and his angels fought against the dragon (satan)*; and the dragon fought and His angels* (the fallen angels).*"*

Verse 8: *"And prevailed not, neither was there found a place any more in heaven."* Time to go!

Verse 9: *"And the great dragon was cast out, that old serpent, called the devil and satan, which deceiveth the whole world: he was cast out onto the earth, and his angels* (fallen angels) *were cast out with Him."*

The events spoken of here are, in my opinion, in the not too distant future. Do not read over the statement, 'which deceiveth the whole world.' God is telling us here that satan as the antichrist will be so convincing that he will deceive the whole world with the exception of a very few, who are the Elect. The Elect are those who know the truth. God sees to it that the Elect know all they need to know about satan's plan of deception. The Elect are charged with exposing this plan to whosoever will listen. That is the purpose of this book; I will expose this evil fraud and his plan, to as many people who will take the time to listen. It is for this reason I say that your soul's well-being depends on knowing the truth. It is far too unlikely that you will ever hear the truths in this book from the pulpit. Some won't speak of them for obvious reasons, but most because they simply do not know. Judgment begins at the pulpit and ignorance will be no excuse on Judgment Day.

Once again, you must understand that satan and his evil angels are "cast" to this earth, and not born of woman, in flesh. I will convince you of this from God's word as we progress in this book. You do not want to be one of those that will be guessing. The time that satan and the fallen angels are allowed to be here is called the Great Tribulation. The time of the Tribulation was seven years, but mercifully in (Mark 13:20), Our Father has shortened that time.

To find out to what length He has shortened it, you will have to keep reading. Let's suffice it to say that it is the best news any believer can get.

Travel through the Creation of this Earth Age

Let's continue in the Book of Genesis, and read verse by verse, with clarification and commentary. In the following you are going to travel through the creation of this earth age. You will read for yourselves things you could spend a lifetime in a pew and never hear from the pulpit.

Genesis 1:3. *"And God said, "Let there be light and there was light."*

John 1:4-5 tells us that Jesus Christ is the Light of the world. Light here = phos, which means underived and absolute, the opposite of darkness. It is used therefore especially for God. The light spoken of in this verse is not the sun. That does not come until verse 14 of the Book of Genesis. This Light is God's SHIKINA GLORY. God spoke and nothing became everything. This is the first day.

Genesis 1:4. *"And God saw the light, that it was good; and God divided the light from the darkness."*

This is light and dark; day and night. This is the first day (2 Peter 3:8). One day to God is 1,000 years to man. God is preparing the earth and is about to put His plan to separate the wheat from the chaff into action. The earth that Our Father loves so much and that has sat void for so long, is about to be rejuvenated.

Genesis 1:5. *"And God called the light day, and the darkness he called night. And the evening and the morning were the 1st day."*

This is the end of the first day in this earth age. Keep in mind that the first earth age is history.

Genesis 1:6. *"And God said, 'Let there be firmament in the midst of the waters, and let it divide the waters from the waters'."*

Firmament here = expanse, something spread out.

Genesis 1:7. *"And God made the firmament, and divided the waters which were under the firmament from the waters which were above the firmament: and it was so."*

The waters that were under the firmament are our ground waters. We use them to this day. Many of us all over the world rely on wells as a source of water. The waters that abide above the firmament are our seas, lakes, rivers and streams.

Genesis 1:8. *"And God called the firmament heaven. And the evening and the morning were the second day."*

Heaven here in Hebrew = high or lofty. This ends the second day. This flesh age is now 2,000 years old.

Genesis 1:9. *"And God said, 'Let the waters under the heaven be gathered together and it was so, unto one place, and let the dry land appear."*

The earth's tectonic plates are being moved. Is this possible? Not long ago a land mass in the Pacific Rim was shifted 5 feet due to an earthquake. This is the formation of the seven continents and the seven seas. In biblical numerics, seven is 'spiritual completeness and perfection.' A witness to this verse is found in Job 38:10-11. You should read this verse for yourself. God is talking to Job here. Proud waves are the oceans. God is sarcastically asking Job if he set the boundaries for the seas. Back to Genesis Ch. 1.

Genesis 1:10. *"And God called the dry land earth; And the gathering together of the waters called He seas: God saw that it was good."*

He called the dry land earth = terrafirma, thus, our terrestrial or earthly bodies in flesh. In 1 Corinthians 15:40 Paul writes.

"There are also celestial bodies, and bodies terrestrial: but the glory of the celestial is one, and the glory of the terrestrial is another."

Make no mistake about it – they are separate and different. Our celestial bodies are not a puff of air – they have mass and substance. Consider the fallen angles. This subject will be covered in depth in chapter 6 of this book.

Genesis 1:11. "And God said, '*Let the earth bring forth grass, the herb yielding seed, and the fruit tree yielding fruit after his kind, whose seed is in itself, upon the earth: and it was so."*

God is creating our food sources. Remember, you are what you eat. Our flesh bodies are organic. We get our minerals from the ground through plants and meat. Animals eat grasses and other plants, and then we eat them. It is all about organics. This is why in the Book of Leviticus, God tells us not to eat scavengers. A scavenger's job is to clean up the earth.

Genesis 1:12. *"And the earth brought forth grass, and herb yielding seed after his (its) kind, and the tree yielding fruit, whose seed was inside itself after his kind: and God saw that it was good."*

Again, this verse is self-explanatory. However, we are seeing that God does like things in order. There are mistakes in this verse. Plants are not people (hims) they are things (its). You will see these kind of mistakes from time to time when reading the Bible and here is why. He, she and it all have the same value in a sentence, it is the subject being talked about that determines the value or in other words, which of the words he, she or it should be used. In this case (it) is the proper choice.

Genesis 1:13. *"And the evening and the morning were the 3rd day."*

God is preparing the earth to be inhabited. Day three of this flesh age is finished.

Genesis 1:14. *"And God said, 'Let there be lights in the firmament of the heaven to divide the day from the night; and let them be for signs and for seasons, and for days and for years."*

God creates the sun and the moon and the stars also, 'for signs and for seasons.' The 12 signs of the zodiac for example do reveal signs and therefore have meaning in God's plan. However, we are never to make a religion out of them. There is a verse in the Book of Job that touches on this. Job 38:12 below.

"Hast thou commanded the morning since thy days; and caused the dayspring to know its place."

"Dayspring" in this verse is the time clock of God's plan for this earth age. If the stars are the spring of the watch, the sun and the moon (marking the days) are the hands of time. This age and this world are not just happenstance. The way the sun revolves around the earth at perfect intervals, marking the years, the hours in the day that divide the months that separate the years, did not just happen. Our Father is telling us exactly who did it. The sun, the moon and the stars did not just fall into their perfect orbits. The big bang theory is in my opinion harder to believe and defend than the creation. Objects in motion tend to stay in motion, in a straight line and not fall into perfect orbits.

Genesis 1:15. *"And let them be for lights in the firmament of the heaven to give light upon the earth, and it was so."*

The sun by day and the moon and stars at night. The stars are used for navigation. This is well known, but Our Father tells us they are for signs as well. He does nothing without telling His children beforehand. How? Through the prophets.

We've covered pretty much all we need, regarding the creation of the sun, the moon and the stars. However, one thing that is important to mention are the place of the sun and moon in prophecy. All prophecy given to us, the children of God, is given in days, or solar, the greater light, the sun. Why? We are God's children, children of light = knowledge. The solar calendar, like God's word, is consistent. It does not change and never will. It will happen exactly as it is written.

Genesis 1:16. *"And God made two great lights; the greater light to rule the day, and the lesser light to rule the night: He made the stars also."*

Genesis 1:17. *"And God set them in the firmament of the heaven to give light upon the earth."*

This is referring to the sun, the moon and the stars.

Genesis 1:18. *"And to rule over the day and over the night, to divide the light from the darkness: and God saw that it was good."*

God is pleased, good in the manuscripts reads, "very good." Our Father loves all of His creation.

Genesis 1:19. *"And the evening and the morning were the 4thday."*

These are God's days, so 4,000 years have passed in this world age. A lot can happen in that amount of time. Where are we,

God's children, during this time? In heaven with Our Father, waiting our turn.

Genesis 1:20. *"And God said let the waters bring forth abundantly the moving creature that have life, and fowl that may fly above the earth in the open firmament of heaven."*

'Firmament of heaven' = high or lofty, as in the expression, 'We aspire to Heavenly heights.' God is starting to create living creatures, such as fish and birds. "Creature" as it is used here is "nephesh" in the original Hebrew language and can be translated "soul." This is the fifth day but as you will see this could go a long way in explaining the ancient cultures such as the Chinese.

Genesis 1:21. *"And God created great whales, and every living creature that moveth, which the waters brought forth abundantly, after their kind, and every winged foul after his kind and God saw that it was good."*

Here is another example of the selection of the words he, she or it. Foul after "his" kind is an obvious error. We know fowl are birds, so it should read "its" kind. Okay, we are making progress. We even have whales now.

Genesis 1:22. *"And God blessed them, saying be fruitful and multiply, and fill the waters in the seas, and let fowl multiply in the earth."*

"In" = on, no problem. God blessed them. God loves his animals as does He all His children.

Genesis 1:23. *"And the evening and the morning were the 5th day."*
This flesh age now has 5,000 years on it. Let us begin the sixth day.

Genesis 1:24. *"And God said, 'Let the earth bring forth the living creature after his kind, cattle and creeping thing, and beast of the earth after his kind: and it was so."*

"Creature" in this verse is translated "nephesh" in the Hebrew language, which means soul. Remember, this is still only the sixth day.

Genesis 1:25. *"And God made the beast of the earth after his kind, and cattle after their kind, and everything that creepeth upon the earth after his kind: and God saw that it was good."*

God is pleased with what he sees. Some of these animals are good to eat, and some are scavengers. A scavenger's job is to clean up the earth, and God instructs us not to eat them. After all, we are what we eat. The book of Leviticus Chapter 11 tells us what we should and shouldn't eat. These are the food laws and yes, they still exist today, documentation Matthew 5:17-18 below, Christ speaking.

"Think not that I have come to destroy the law, or the prophets: I am (have) *not come to destroy, but to fulfill. For verily* (Truly) *I say unto you, till heaven and earth pass, not one jot or one title shall pass from the law, till all be fulfilled."*

A "jot" is the smallest character in the Hebrew language. It looks like this: ' , and its purpose is to change the sound of a word, say from a long "a" to a soft "a." Christ, in this verse, is telling us that the food laws are still in effect.

Many use Acts Chapter 10 to teach the falsehood that the food laws are no longer need be enforced. This is a great example as to why it is so important to pick up the subject. The subject in Acts Chapter 10 and part of Chapter 11 is "the gentiles." We are not to call the "gentiles" common (unclean). In other words, what God was saying is, that since Christ's sacrifice on the cross, "salvation" is open to everyone, John 3:16 below.

"For God so loved the world, that He gave His only begotten Son, that whosoever believeth in Him should not perish, but have everlasting life."

Don't worry, eating scavengers will not damn you to hell, but like smoking, they will make you sick.

Genesis 1:26. *"And God said, 'Let Us make man in our image, and after our likeness: and let them have dominion over the fish of the sea, and over the foul of the air, and over the cattle and over all the earth, and over every creeping thing that creepeth upon the earth'."*

Okay, sharpen up for me. This is important. We are still on day six. It is the sixth day, and God is about to create man. This is going to be an example of why it is so important to read the Bible, chapter by chapter and verse by verse, always staying with the subject and always determining the time frame. It is important to note that man is created last here. Why? So that the "heretics" could not say that any "mortal" man had a part in creation. There are several words for "man" in the Hebrew language and you must understand the difference.

The word "Adam" by itself, without the article "Eth-Ha," means "mankind," all mankind in general. Because there is no article we now know we are talking about "all mankind" in this verse. Later, on in the eighth day, we will see the name 'Eth-Ha-'Adam,' which with the article 'Eth-Ha' means "The Adam", or in English, "The Man," referring to "The Adam" of Adam and Eve. The distinction is important in that Eth-Ha-Adam is the man through which Christ would come, umbilical cord to umbilical cord through Mother Eve. But for now, we are talking about the sixth day creation.

Let's go ahead and break this verse down. "Let us," God is talking to the angels, us. The word in the Hebrew language is "Elohim." This means 'God and the angels.' Remember, we were in our angelic bodies at that time and with Him in heaven. God's plan for salvation requires that all souls be born in flesh, in this, the second earth age. "Image and likeness." These words together mean "exactly." The word in Hebrew is "phantom." It means "mirrored image." The point is, in our flesh bodies we look exactly as we do in our celestial bodies. This answers the question "will we recognize our loved ones in heaven?" Yes. Physically speaking, there doesn't appear to be all that much difference either. The Israelites ate "manna," angel's food, when they wondered for 40 years in the wilderness, as depicted in Exodus 16:35.

"And the children of Israel (the Israelites) *did eat manna forty years, until they came to a land inhabited; they did eat manna, until they came onto the borders of the land of Canaan."*

"Manna" in the Hebrew language means "what's that." It is also called "angel's food," and it fell from heaven, documentation, Psalms 78:23-25.

"Though He had commanded the clouds from above, and opened the doors of heaven. And had rained down "manna" upon them to eat, and had given them of the corn of heaven.
Man did eat angel's food; He sent them "meat to the full."

"Meat" here is "quail." It also fell from heaven.

Let us go back to Exodus 16:31. This verse describes the way it looked and tasted. It was white, flaky and wafer like with a taste like honey. This is the heaven sent nourishment that sustained the Israelites "forty years," and they were healthy and fine. Forty years is far longer than the FDA tests anything today. The point here is that flesh man did eat angel's food and visa versa. Oh yes, it works the other way as well. Shortly after the crucifixion Christ appeared to the Apostles and asked if they had any meat. Let's start with Luke 24:30 and document that Christ is in His angelic body.

"Behold my hands and my feet, that is I myself, (it's me)*: Handle Me and see; for a spirit* (ghost) *hath not flesh and bones as you*

see me have."

Christ is telling them that our other bodies (He is in His) are not puffs of air. They have mass. If you read on, note that they still did not get it, even after He had given them an example of this on the Mount of Transfiguration when He was yet with them, Luke 24:41, Christ speaking.

"He said unto them, have you any meat?"

There you have it, directly from God's word. Recall of this information will be crucial when satan and the fallen angels return to this earth. Very soon! They will not look like "little green men" from outer space. Satan will look like what you think Christ looks like and will be claiming to be Christ. The fallen angels will look like royalty. Be prepared. It is written. It will happen. Let's continue in Genesis as God creates men.

Genesis 1:27. *"So God created man in His own image, and in the image of God created He Him; male and female created he them."*

Read this verse very carefully because there are those who believe that this verse is the creation of men only. The "Him" being spoken of here is Jesus Christ, "Emmanuel," which translated means, "God with us" in flesh. *"Man in His own image and in the image of God created He Him."* Note that "His, He and Him" are capitalized. This reverence is reserved for God. Who looks and acts like God? Jesus Christ, God with us in a flesh body. The others being created here are flesh men (mankind). The 6th day creation. We all look like ourselves whether in angelic or flesh bodies. We have traits like God Our Father only in as much as He is Our Father. Do we not have the traits of our flesh parents? Saint John records Christ as saying in, John 14:9.

"He that hath seen Me hath seen the Father."

Why? Because they look alike (exactly alike) in either body. Again, Jesus Christ is our Heavenly Father in a flesh body. Your documentation can be found in two places in The New Testament. In the book of Matthew, Matthew means "God's Gift." Matthew 1:23 reads.

"Behold a virgin shall be with child, and shall bring forth a son, and they shall call His name Emmanuel." (Which interpreted means, *"God with us."*

This next verse is prophesy of this event fulfilled from the Old Testament. Isaiah 7:14 states.

'"Therefore the Lord Himself shall give you a sign; Behold a virgin shall conceive and bear a son, and shall His name be 'Immanuel."'

This verse was written 1000 years before Christ was born. It is for this reason and many more like it that confirm the Bibles credibility. The difference in the spelling of Immanuel here and in the Book of Matthew is easily explained. The Old Testament was written, for the most part, in Hebrew, and the New Testament in Greek. By the way, don't ever believe anyone who tells you that the Old Testament does not apply to us today, because it does. The Apostle Timothy states in 2 Timothy 3:16.

"All scripture is given by inspiration of God, and is profitable for doctrine (truth), *for reproof* (proof), *for correction* (guidance), *for instruction and righteousness."*

The lessons and admonitions of the Old Testament are for us today. Paul tells us in 1 Corinthians 10:11.

"Now all these things happened to them as an ensamples (examples); and they are written for our admonition (warning), upon whom the end of the world has come."

According to Ecclesiastes 1:9, we have covered it before, so to paraphrase, there is nothing new under the sun, and history will always repeat itself. Our Father loves His children (us) so very much that He also took on a flesh body. Why? One, He wouldn't put us through something He Himself was not willing to go through, and He served as an example showing us how it is done. Do not ever accuse God of not being fair. It is always a wise idea to take inventory of yourself. Note the remainder of this verse, *"Male and female created He them."* These are the people of the sixth day creation. It is unlikely you have ever heard of this so let us read the next verse and listen closely to the instructions God gives to these children. Careful reading will reveal yet more evidence of the first earth age. Not knowing the truth about the beginning of that age will make it impossible for anyone to understand how it is going to come down in these end days.

Genesis 1:28: *"And God blessed them and God said unto them, be fruitful and multiply, and "replenish" the earth, and subdue it! And have dominion over the fish of the sea, and over the fowl of the air, and over every living thing that moveth upon the earth."*

God blesses His sixth day creation and tells them to "multiply" (procreate) and "REPLENISH" the earth. Webster's dictionary defines "replenish" as: To add to something; (procreate) "to replace what has gone or been used." In this case what has (is) "gone" are the souls that inhabited the earth during the first earth age. There was a first earth age and there were "inhabitants" on this earth in that age.

Genesis 1:29. *"And God said, 'Behold I have given you every herb bearing seed, which is upon the face of all the earth, and every tree in which is the fruit of the tree yielding seed; to you it shall be for meat.'"* (food).

"Every tree" is okay to eat from. I am sure that if there is an apple tree, it is all right to eat from it. This is still the sixth day.

Genesis 1:30. *"And to every beast of the earth, and to every foul of the air, and to everything that creepeth on the earth wherein there is life. I have given every herb for meat: and 'it was so'."*

"Life" as it is used here = "Nephesh." In Hebrew it means "the breath that is life." (Soul)!

Genesis 1:31. *"And God saw everything he had made, and behold, it was "very good" and the evening and the morning were the 6th day."*

God looks over the sixth day of creation. Notice that He says it is "VERY GOOD." God loves all his children. He may not like what we're doing sometimes, but He does love us, all of us. He took on a flesh body the same as us. Christ, God in a flesh body, died on the cross for our sins, "salvation," where upon repentance, our sins are forgiven. They are not just forgiven, they are "blotted" out as if they never existed, and God forgets them. He does this not only for our sake but for His as well, as we read in Isaiah 43:25, God speaking:

"I even I am He that blotteth out thy transgressions for mine own sake, and I will not remember thy sins." Repent and your slate is clean.

Part II

Genesis 2:1. *"Thus the heavens and the earth were finished, and all the hosts of them."*

"Hosts" = all the inhabitants on the earth now and those who were in heaven waiting to be born. Heavens is plural and earth, singular. Why? God destroyed the first earth age and there is only one earth.

Genesis 2:2 *"And on the 7th day God ended His work which He had made: and He rested on the seventh (7) day from all His work which He had made."*

This is the seventh day. Seven in biblical numbers is spiritual completeness and spiritual perfection. All is good and 'God rests.' Christ is our Sabbath today. We are to take our rest in Him every day not just one day of the week. As is typical with man, he clouds the issue. This is well documented in the book of Mark. Mark was a young lad when he followed Christ. His gospel is fast moving and vivacious. He was an enthusiastic follower of Christ. For his trouble, horses dragged him until he was dead. Mark 7:13 reads.

"Making the word of God of none effect through your traditions, which you have delivered: and many such like things do you." God doesn't like it. Sabbath means rest.

In Mark 2:27-8, Christ speaks, saying.

"And He said unto them, the Sabbath was made for man, not man for the Sabbath." Sabbath means rest. Verse 28.

"Therefore the son of man is also the Lord of the Sabbath."

As is usually the case, man has it wrong. The Sabbath is for man's benefit, not Christ's. We are to take our rest (peace of mind) in Christ every day, not just one day of the week. These are truly words to live by.

Genesis 2:3. *"And God blessed the seventh day, and sanctified it: because that in it He had rested from all His work which God creates and made."*

This ends the seventh day. Back to the Book of Genesis.

Genesis 2:4. *"These are the generations of the heavens and of the Earth when they were created in the day that the Lord God made the earth and the heavens."*

Generations = pedigree or family history.

Genesis 2:5. *"And every plant of the field before it was in the earth, and every herb of the field before it grow: for the Lord God had not caused it to rain upon the earth, and there was not a man to till the ground."*

God is looking for a farmer. Our Father loves agriculture and alludes to it frequently in his word.

Genesis 2:6. *"But there went up a mist from the earth and watered the whole face of the ground."*

God causes it to rain.

Genesis 2:7. *"And the Lord God formed man of the dust of the ground and breathes into his nostrils the breath of life."*

This is now the eighth day. There have been men and women moving about the earth for more than 1,000 years. Note that God "forms" this man as potter forms clay. My point? He gave special care in creating this man. Why not, he is Eth-Ha Adam, as advertised, "The Man," through which Christ would come, umbilical cord to umbilical cord through Mother Eve.

This makes The Adam of Adam and Eve the great-great-great....... grandfather of Jesus Christ, does it not? It does, and you will find the documentation in the book of Luke. The apostle Luke was a medical doctor who sometimes scribed for Paul, the author of most of the New Testament. It is believed that Paul had very poor eye site as a result of his experience on the road to Damascus. Consequentially Luke and perhaps other apostles recorded for Paul. Luke, for his efforts to spread God's word, was hanged. It was a dangerous time to be a Christian in the Middle East. Come to think of it, it was a lot like today, wasn't it? *"Nothing New under the sun."* Luke 3:23-38 gives us a complete account of Christ's lineage.

This account is actually Mary's pedigree and therefore Joseph's in-laws. Notice in verse 38.

"Which was the son of Enos, which was the son of Seth (the second son of Adam and Eve after Abel was killed), *which was the son of Adam,"* ('eth ha' Adam). The idiom, "The breath of life," in the Hebrew language is 'neshamah', "The breath that is life."

Genesis 2:8. *"And the Lord God planted a garden eastward of Eden: and there he put the man who he had formed."*

Where was this garden? Somewhere between the Tigress and the Euphrates rivers. This is a real location on this earth remember, this is a "real world" study, not a collection of fairy tales.

Genesis 2:9. *"And out of the ground made the Lord God to grow every tree that is pleasant to the sight and good for food; the 'tree of life' also in the midst of the garden, and the tree of* (the) *knowledge of good and evil."*

There are trees in the garden for food, no doubt, but there are two trees mentioned here that need some explanation. The tree of "life" here is Jesus Christ, where in belief upon Him lies 'life eternal.' If you don't believe in Christ you are 'spiritually dead.' Your soul, which is to go into your eternal body, is in danger of dying. No soul, no life in your eternal body. Then you also have in the garden, the tree of (with) "the knowledge of good and evil," which is simply a metaphor for satan himself. Yes satan was in the Garden of Eden as was documented earlier using the book of Job. A tree is an apt metaphor (comparison) for a man. A man has a trunk, a torso. He has limbs, arms and even a crotch. Satan has never and will never be in a flesh body. He will "never" be born of women innocent, with no recollection of the first earth age. Satan hates God, and God knows it. The controversy in this age is between God and satan. Satan has and will always have all the knowledge of "good and evil," and everything that happened in the first earth age. It is quite likely he (and the fallen angels) know you by name, and they know your weaknesses and they intend to work on that nerve. If for no other reason, this is why you need to understand the Bible, not only for the history, but also for its prophesies. Much of the bible is like reading tomorrow's newspaper. What you need to remember from this verse is that satan is in the garden on this earth, in this earth age, and that spells trouble.

Genesis 2:10. *"And a river went out of Eden to water the garden: and from thence it was parted, and became into four heads."*
Location, location, location.

Genesis 2:11. *"The name of the first is Pison: that is it which compasseth the whole land of Havilah where there is gold."*

Pison is west of the Euphrates River.

Genesis 2:12. *"And the gold of that land is good: there is Bdellium and the Onyx Stone."*

There are riches there. Maybe this is why satan has an interest here. We will find out gold and precious stones are not the only things that have his attention.

Genesis 2:13. *"And the name of the second river is Gihon: the same is that compasseth the whole land of Ethiopia."*

Genesis 2:14. *"And the name of the third river is Hinnekel: that is which goeth towards the east of Assyria. And the fourth river is Euphrates."*

Now we have it. We have fixed a location. The areas mentioned here, for the most part still exist today.

Genesis 2:15. *"And the Lord God took the man and put him into the Garden of Eden to dress it and to keep it."*

This is Eth-Ha-Adam, "The man Adam." This Adam is a "husbandman" which means "farmer." Adam's job is to work the grounds and tend to the garden. Although our focus is on the Garden, there are other people on the earth at this time and they are busy doing their thing. Genesis 2:16.

"And the Lord God commands the man, saying, "of every tree of the garden thou mayest freely eat."

Now, sharpen up. God tells Adam that he may eat of "all" the trees in the garden. This means it is okay to eat from the apple trees, if there are any there. It is time to do away with the fairy tale that is taught about Eve and the apple in the garden. Did you know the word "apple" doesn't even appear in the book of Genesis? Let's keep reading and discover what "the sin in the Garden of Eden" really was.

Genesis 2:17. *"And of the tree of "the knowledge of good and evil" (satan), thou shall not eat of it. For in the day thou eatest there of thou shalt surely die."*

We've established that the "tree of the knowledge of good and evil" is satan, "the serpent," "that Old dragon," "the devil," "the little horn," "Lucifer," "that man of sin," "the son of perdition" (death). These are all names for satan but there is only one. God does not want Adam to have anything to do with Satan. Why? Satan wants to pollute the line through which Christ will come, thus averting his own destruction. Satan is a liar in John 8: 44. Christ tells us.

"Satan is a liar and the father of it."

Satan, through deception, wants to cause the death of as many of our souls as he can. He believes if he can get enough souls, God will have to change his plan and not destroy him. You do not want to be one of the souls satan deceives, as there is a heavy penalty for this.

Genesis 2:18. *"And the Lord said it is not good that "the man" should be alone; I will make him a help meet for him."*

Notice God refers to Adam as "The Man" – we covered this. Adam is a farmer. God knows he will need some help around the farm. Meet = counterpart, as in "help."

Genesis 2:19. *"And out of the ground God formed every beast of the field, and every foul of the air; and brought them unto Adam to see what he would call them: And whatsoever Adam called every living creature that was the name there of."*

God in this verse creates the "domestic animals," farm animals; horses to pull the plow, chickens, cows, rabbits. You get the idea. After all, Adam is a husbandman (farmer), a tiller of the ground.

Genesis 2:20. *"And Adam gave names to all the cattle, and to the foul of the air, and every beast of the field."*

As Our Father instructed him to do in Genesis 2:21, 22, and 23.

"And the Lord God caused a deep sleep to fall upon Adam and he slept: and he took one of Adam's ribs, and closed up the flesh there of."

Could this be the first surgery in this earth age? Men and women have the same number of ribs. Don't just take my word for it – ask a doctor. So what is really going on here? Fifty years ago, this would be impossible to understand, but with the discovery of the helix curve (DNA) it is now understandable. The word "rib" in the Hebrew language is translated "curve" as in "helix curve." God took Adam's feminine DNA and created Eve from it. Thus, in verse 23 Eve is bone of Adam's bone and flesh of his flesh. This is not a stretch – man is able to clone. This knowledge brings a verse, written some 6000 years ago to the real world of today. This verse is but one reason the Bible is said to be "pregnant."

Genesis 2:24. *"Therefore shall a man leave his father and his mother, and shall cleave unto his wife: and they shall be one flesh."*

Did you know God was married once? He married Jerusalem figuratively speaking, which we find in Ezekiel 16:8, with God speaking.

"Now when I passed by thee, and looked upon thee, behold, thy time was the time of love; and I spread my skirt over thee (Jerusalem), *and covered thy nakedness: ya I swear unto thee, and entered into a covenant with thee, saith the Lord God, and thou becamest mine."*

Our Father spread His skirt over Jerusalem, the symbolic act back then and even today in some places of the world, signifying the taking under one's protection, still common in the east for marrying. Also, did you know God is a divorcee? Jeremiah 3:8 states.

"And I saw, when for all the causes where by backsliding Israel (not the geographic location, but God's Elect) *committed adultery* (idolatry*), I had put her away, and given Her a bill of divorce:"'*

Is this in God's law? Yes, as we can see in Deuteronomy 24:1.

"When a man hath taken a wife, and married Her, and it comes to pass that she finds no favor in His eyes, because He hath found

some uncleanness in Her: then let Him write Her a bill of divorcement, and give it in Her hand, and send Her out of His house."

The book of Deuteronomy, written by Moses, is about God's law, and we have previously documented that Christ did not do away with the law. The point I want to make here is that mankind, in flesh, makes mistakes. There is only one unpardonable sin, and that has not been committed. The fact is, it cannot be committed until the antichrist sits in the temple claiming to be Christ. This subject will be covered in depth later in this book. What God wants you to take away from this is - do not let anyone treat you like a second-class citizen just because you have been divorced. Not a priest, pastor, minister or friend. Divorce is not the unpardonable sin and forgiveness is for everyone. Christ's sacrifice on the cross ushered in our current dispensation of grace, where upon one's repentance, our sins are forgiven. Not only are they forgiven, but Our Father says, 'He doesn't want to hear of them again.' Repent, hit the delete button and move on. Remember, Christ is the one who forgives sin, not some man, according to John 8:32.

"And the truth shall make you free." God's word does not put us in bondage.

Genesis 2:25. *"And they were both naked, the man and his wife. And they were not ashamed."*

They were young and innocent. Satan is going to change this in the next chapter of Genesis. You do not want to miss this.

Part III

Genesis 3:1. *"Now the serpent was more subtle than any beast of the field which the Lord God had made. And he said unto the woman* (Eve), *"Yea, hath God said, Ye shall not eat of everything of the garden?"*

"Serpent" we know is just another name for satan, the devil. "Serpent" is one of as many as twelve names satan goes by. Satan is a "man" (ish) which in the original Hebrew manuscripts "supernatural man," not a "mortal man" (Adam). Let's be perfectly clear – we are not talking about a snake here. Satan is on this earth, in the Garden of Eden, and is in an angelic body, or better said, a celestial body, at the time of this verse. An angelic body is however, not a puff of air. An angelic, celestial, spiritual, or eternal body (they are all the same body), as documented, has substance and mass.

A snake cannot talk, but the power of tradition (traditions of men; fairy tales) have given us in our minds a picture of a snake, a woman and an apple, the former by interpretation and the latter by invention. It is a fairy tale, and it is simply not what happened. Why is it so important to know the truth? If you don't know how it was in the beginning, you will never be able to comprehend how it comes down in the end time, the very times we are living in. Again, the word 'apple' does not appear anywhere in the book of Genesis.

"Subtle" = wise. Satan is very wise and beautiful (Ezekiel 28:3 & 12). God states *"perfect in beauty."* Satan is not the ugly horned demon as you have been falsely taught. We are going to go real world on this. Using God's word and only God's word, we are going to find out what really happened.

WHAT WAS THE SIN IN THE GARDEN?

Genesis 3:2. *"And the woman said unto the serpent* (satan), *we may eat of the fruit of the trees of the garden."*

Eve is talking face to face with satan in this verse. Put yourself in her shoes (feet) for a moment. She, while going about her day in the paradise that is the garden, now finds herself face to face with the devil himself. Eve is a young woman, probably about fourteen, and now is eye-to-eye with the "father of lies." You may be thinking, she should have run, I would have. Would you have? If you're reading this, you are probably one of God's Elect. If you are, you may very well get your chance to meet satan face-to-face when He returns to this earth as antichrist in the not too distant future. Never forget this. Satan is a beautiful looking being, *"the full pattern,"* perhaps even mesmerizing. Think about it. His appearance does not frighten Eve. Whatever the case, he has Eve's undivided attention. She may be a little flustered in that she omits from the command of God, in Genesis 2:16, the word "freely." This omission is just enough doubt for the devil to go to work on her. Eve continues.

Genesis 3:3:.*"But the fruit of the tree which is in the midst of the garden, God hath said, 'ye shall not eat of it, neither shall ye "touch" it, lest ye die'."*

Eve is talking about the tree of "the knowledge of good and evil" (satan), that God spoke of back in Genesis 2:7. Eve is totally unaware of who she is talking to. The word "touch" used here in this verse, in the Hebrew language is "naga" which means "to lie with a woman," as in a "sexual act." It's word #5060 in your Strong's Concordance. Do not just take my word for it, check it out for yourself. *"Lest you die,"* not instantly, though. Satan is death, however, God was talking about a spiritual death, the death of a soul. Satan is not really lying here because he is talking about a physical death. There are two deaths documented in the Bible and they covered in-depth in chapter eight of this book.

A statement like this is what makes satan so dangerous – he mixes lies with truth. In Revelation 20:6.

"Blessed and holy is he that hath part in the first resurrection: on

such the second death hath no power."

The first death is the death of your flesh body. Everyone born in a flesh body will experience this death. The second death however, is the death of your soul. This is the death you want to avoid at all cost. This is undoubtedly the reason Christ said in Matthew 10:28.

"And fear not them which kill the body (flesh body), *but are not able to kill the soul: but rather fear him which is able to destroy soul and body in hell."*

Your soul is the thing that makes you, you. It is your intellect, your spirit. When we die, our souls return instantly into our eternal bodies and back with Our Father from where they came and is documented in the Book of Ecclesiastes 12:6-7. 2 Corinthians 6-8 describes this fact in detail.

"Therefore we are always confident, knowing that, while we are at home in the (flesh) *body, we are absent from the Lord. For we walk by faith, not by sight. We are confident I say, well pleased that to be absent from the body (flesh), is to be present with the Lord."*

Make no mistake; no one who has ever died is in some hole in the ground. They are back home with Our Father, safe and sound. This fact comes right from God Himself. *"God is not the God of the dead but of the living."* Again with Genesis with Eve talking to the devil;

Genesis 3:4. *"And the serpent said unto the woman, ye shall not surely die:"*

Here again, satan is doing what he does best, twist the truth.

Genesis 3:5. *"For God doth know that in the day ye eat thereof, then your eyes shall be opened, and ye shall be as gods* (lower case), *knowing good and evil."*

"Ye shall be as gods," (lower case g) is a flat out lie!

There is only one God. But the other two statements are accurate. Keep in mind satan is the "tree with the knowledge of good and evil."

Genesis 3:6. *"And when the woman saw that the tree was good for food and that it was pleasant to the eye, and a tree to be desired to make one wise, she took the fruit thereof, and did eat, and gave also unto her husband, with her and he did eat."*

First, we are not talking about a tree here; we are talking about a supernatural being (ish), satan, aka that old serpent. Eve was not "repelled" by satan's looks. On the contrary, she states that the tree (satan) is "pleasant" to look at. In the Hebrew language, it is "chamad"= delightful; "delectable thing." We would say today, "not too hard on the eyes." or that he was "yummy." Nothing new under the sun is going on here. *"As it was in the beginning so shall it be in the end."* Tree is just a metaphor. The "food" being talked about here is "knowledge." Satan is very wise. Why? Once again, he has all the knowledge of the first earth age. No doubt he has knowledge of God's plan for salvation, as well. That plan is why he is interested in Eve. Remember, Eve is to be the mother of Christ, umbilical cord to umbilical cord. Satan knows this and is trying to pollute the bloodline through which Christ, The Savior, would come, destroying redemption and thereby avoiding His own doom: Or so he believes. The last part of verse 6,

"She took the fruit thereof, and did eat."

This is the real sin in the garden. Eve took the fruit of satan's "loins." Stated plainly, Satan had "sex" with Eve. Apparently, Adam got involved, also. This may shock some, but this is the "TRUTH" and is well documented in God's word. It just takes a little work to get at the truth. Please keep reading. Your chance at the Eternity may very well depend on it.

Genesis 3:7. *"And the eyes of them* (Adam and Eve) *both were opened, and they knew* (realized) *that they were naked; and they sewed fig leaves together, and made themselves aprons."*

Adam and Eve noticed they were naked. Their eyes are opened, and they covered their private parts. They did not use the aprons to cover their mouths, because they did not eat an apple.

Genesis 3:8. *"And they heard the voice of the Lord God walking in the garden in the cool of the day; and Adam and his wife hid themselves from the presence of the Lord God amongst the trees of the garden."*

They were scared and ashamed. They had disobeyed God's command. Do not read over the statement, *"in the cool of the day."* The location of the garden is in the desert, yet it is cool during the day, and why not? It was designed to be paradise on earth, but not for long.

Genesis 3:9. *"And the Lord God called unto Adam and said unto him, "Where art thou?"*

I have a feeling God knows.

Genesis 3:10. *"And he said, I heard thy voice in the garden and I was afraid, because I was naked and I hid myself."*

There's no point in lying now.

Genesis 3:11. *"And He* (God) *said, 'who told thee that thou wast naked? Hast thou eaten of the tree wherefore I commanded thee that thou shouldest not eat?"*

Genesis 3:12. *"And the man said, the woman who thou gavest to be with me, she gave me of the tree, and I did eat."*
Nothing new under the sun is here. Adam is passing the buck.

Genesis 3:13. *"And the Lord said to the woman, 'What is this that thou hast done?' And the woman said, 'The serpent beguiled me, and I did eat.'"*

The word "beguiled" in the Greek language is "expatio," which means "wholly seduced." It is #1818 in the Strong's Concordance of the Bible. You have to give Eve credit here – she is being honest. Unfortunately, the worst is not over by a long shot. Paul uses the word beguiled in the new testament to describe this sin in the Garden in 2 Corinthians 11:3. Paul is warning those in the church at Corinth about satan's inevitable return.

"But I fear, lest by any means, as the serpent "beguiled" Eve through his subtilty, so your minds should be corrupted from the simplicity that is Christ."

Our Fathers word is so smoothly sewn together.

Genesis 3:14. *"And the Lord God said unto the serpent* (satan*), because thou hast done this, thou are cursed above all the cattle, and above every beast of the field; upon thy belly thou shalt go, and dust shalt thou eat all the days of thy life."*

God curses satan, who quite frankly I am surprised is still standing there. Notice God asks no questions of satan. There is no parley, no exchange. Why? God knows satan is a liar. There is no need to hear his side of this. Sentence is pronounced immediately. *"Upon thy belly"* is a figure of speech. The words imply the utmost humiliation. In Psalms 44:25, "upon thy belly" is a figure of utter defeat, and in Psalms 72:8, as in eats dust all the days of his life. What a snake.

Genesis 3:15. *"And I will put enmity between thee* (satan) *and the woman, and between thy seed* (satan's seed) *and her seed (Eves seed); it shall bruise thy head and thou shall bruise his heel."*

This is the first prophesy in the Bible. "Enmity" = "Hatred." Not just hatred between satan and Mother Eve, but hatred between satan's seed (sperma) = (his offspring's children), and Adam and Eve's children. Why mention satan's offspring? Eve is pregnant with satan's child. You could not write a soap opera better than this. The truth is truly stranger than fiction. Before you throw my book down, please just read the next verse:

Genesis 3:16. *"Unto the woman he said, 'I will greatly multiply thy sorrow and thy conception; in sorrow thou shalt bring forth children; and thy desire shall be unto thy husband, and he shall rule over thee.'"*

Here is your proof. *"Unto the woman" l*eaves no doubt that God is talking to Eve. The word "conception" can only mean one thing. Eve is going to have a baby. The NIV says instead of "conception," "childbearing," which leaves room for doubt. The *King James* is very clear. Eve is pregnant. You may be inclined to say, "maybe it's Adams," and you would be right, half right, anyway. The fact is, Eve, because of the aforementioned encounter, is pregnant with both Adam's and satan's baby. Is this possible? Yes, it is a medical fact. *"Multiply thy sorrow,"* "Sorrows" = "birth pains." It is #6093 in your Strong's Concordance of the *Bible*. Satan seduced young Eve, and Adam got involved, also. These are God's words, not mine. A witness to this event can be found in The New Testament. In 2 Corinthians 11:3.

Genesis 3:17. *"And unto Adam he said, "because thou hast hearkened unto the voice of thy wife, and hast eaten of the tree of which I have command thee, saying, thou shalt not eat of it; cursed is the ground for thy sake; in sorrow thou shalt eat of it all the days of thy life."*

There would be no more paradise for these two. Used here, "sorrow" = pain. Adam is a farmer. God is telling Adam that he is going to have to work hard for his living. Naturally, because Adam is a farmer, he is going to face Mother Nature, and she is fickle. Like the farmers of today, he will have to work physically as well as smartly.

Genesis 3:18. *"Thorns also and thistles shall it bring forth to thee; and thou shalt eat the herb of the field."*

Adam is going to have to work for it, but the ground will produce for him.

Genesis 3:19. *"In the sweat of thy face shalt thou eat bread, till thou return to the ground; For out of it wast thou taken: For dust thou art, and unto dust thou shall return."*

Because of his part in this transgression, Adam will have to grow crops by the sweat of his brow and all the hardships that come with the job – weather issues, weeds, stony ground, insects, blights, etc. Adam was formed from the ground, and his flesh body, when he is done with it (he dies), will go back to the ground from where it came, and his soul will go instantly back to the Father. You will need to keep in mind the definition of heaven, "wherever God is."

Genesis 3:20. *"And Adam called his wife's name Eve; because she was the mother of all living."*

"Eve" in the Hebrew language means "living." Eve is called 'the mother of all living' in this verse. This verse, without being properly explained, is used by many to teach the falsehood that Adam and Eve were the first human beings to walk the earth in this earth age. Having read this far, you know this belief is not true. So what is the explanation? This verse is talking "spiritually" alive, as in your “soul.” We have documented that there are “two deaths.” One is of your flesh body and the other of your soul, or “spiritual” being (body).

Let me explain. Eve is the mother of Christ, umbilical cord to umbilical cord. Christ, “Emmanuel,” which means 'God with us,' died on the cross, whereby believing upon “Him” and His power to forgive, your soul is saved (John 3:16). If you do not believe in Christ and his power to forgive sins, you have no hope of making the Eternity.

But, because God took on a flesh body and was crucified, our sins, upon repentance, are forgiven. “Repentance” = a “true change of heart” (Isaiah 43:25). When God forgives our transgressions, He does not want to hear about them again! Why? It shows Him that you doubt that what He suffered on the cross was enough. When you doubt, it is like re-crucifying Christ all over again. God forgives and forgets, but we remember. Why? So we don’t do it again. Lose the guilt, but keep the experience. This is wisdom.

Genesis 3:21. *“Unto Adam also and his wife did the Lord God make coats of skin, and clothed them.”*

God has handed out their punishments. As you can see, He still loves and cares for them. God loves His children. He may not like what we do sometimes, but He loves “all” His family.

Genesis 3:22. *“And the Lord God said, behold the man has become one of us, to know good and evil: now, lest he put forth his hand, and take also of the tree of life (Christ), and eat, and live forever.”*

God is talking to “us” in this verse – you, me and many others. At the time all of this is going on, the rest of us are still in heaven with Him waiting our turn. While we were with Him in heaven, we still had full knowledge of the first earth age. It isn’t until it’s our turn to be born in flesh, innocent, that we lose that knowledge. It is quite likely satan has told Adam and Eve many secrets of the first earth age. There can be no doubt that he has made God look like the bad guy. Adam and Eve will have to seek out the truth for themselves, the same as you and I. We have to take the first step. This is the true meaning of "Seek and you shall find." This pearl of wisdom is not talking about a coin. If you lose something, it is okay to ask God for help finding it, but that is not the subject of the verse. What is important to Him is that you gain the "knowledge" you need to insure the salvation of your soul.

Genesis 3:23. *"Therefore, the Lord God sent him from the Garden of Eden, to till the ground from wence he was taken."*
God sends Adam packing and Eve, with him.

Genesis 3:24. *"So He drove out the man; and He placed at the east of the Garden of Eden a Cherubim, and a flaming sword which turned every way, to keep the way of the Tree of Life."*

"Cherubim" = guards. To guide the way of the Tree of Life (Christ) and preserve the hope of salvation for a ruined creation (Genesis 2:15). A flaming sword = God's two-edged sword, the sword of truth that cuts both ways and burns those who are against God documentation (Revelation 1:16).

Genesis 4:1. *"And Adam knew his wife: and she conceived and bore Cain and said I have gotten a man from the Lord."*

Better said, "Adam had known his wife" back in (Genesis 3:6). Satan "knew"= (beguiled) Eve, also. We know there was a conception (Genesis 3:17). Grasping this truth will allow us to understand fully what is going on. Eve is about to give birth as a result of the action in the garden. Eve is about to give birth to Cain. Cain was the first murderer, and that makes sense, because satan is Cain's father. John 8:44 documents this. Christ talking,

"You are of your father the devil, and the lusts of your father you

will do. He was a murderer from the beginning, and abode not in the truth, because there is no truth in him. When he speaketh a lie, he speaketh of his own: for he is a liar and the father of it."

Yes, Cain is satan's spawn, and Cain's children are called "Kenites." The Kenites are mentioned numerous times in the Bible but one stands out. It is 1 Chronicles 2:55:

"And the families of the scribes which dwell at Jabez; The Tirathites, the Shameathites and Sachathites. These are the "Kenites" that came of Hemath, the father of the house of Rechab."

A little deeper study of this verse will let you know that the "offspring of Cain" who is the son of the devil became "scribes" (record keepers). You do not want the devil's children keeping the books – it is just asking for trouble. This information goes a long way to explaining some of the mistakes in the Bible. Eventually, the Kenites did take over the task of keeping the records for a while, and that caused obvious problems.

Genesis 4:2. *"And she "again" bore his brother, Abel. And Abel was a keeper of sheep, but Cain was a tiller of the ground."*

This is important so sharpen up. "Again," in the Hebrew language means "to continue in something." It is not much of a stretch in the English language either, as in "Do it 'again,' (continue). In this case, Eve is "continuing" in labor. If a woman continues in labor, she is having twins. Yes, Cain and Abel are twins. Is it possible to have twins by two different fathers? The answer is yes. Ask a doctor. Cain and Abel were twins. Cain of satan and Abel of Eth-Ha-Adam. This makes the point that supernatural beings, those in their angelic bodies, not only have mass but have the ability to reproduce. This is an important point and will come up again when we get to the influx of the fallen angels.

Genesis 4:3. *"And in the process of time it came to pass, that Cain brought of the fruit of the ground an offering unto the Lord."*

Cain is a farmer.

Genesis 4:4. *"And Abel, he also brought of the firstlings of his flock and of the fat thereof. And the Lord had respect unto Abel and to his offering."*

Abel raised sheep. He brought God the best of his herd, as God requires. Cain did not offer his best. This is not a surprise considering who his father is. More importantly is that Cain and Abel brought their offerings at the same time. *"And in the process of time."* In the manuscripts it says, *"at a place and time appointed."* Why is this important? Because they brought their offerings at the same time, note the word, "also." If they brought their offerings at the same time, which was tradition, they also would have to be the same age. Again, they are twins. "Conceived" in the activity back in Genesis 3:6.

Genesis 4:5. *"But unto Cain and his offering He* (God) *had no respect. And Cain was very wroth, and his countenance fell."*

In other words. God asks Cain, why are you so angry and why is your face beet red? God had no respect for Cain's offering. Why? Cain had no respect for God. Cain was angry and his face turned red with that anger.

Genesis 4:6. *"And the Lord said unto Cain, Why art thou wroth? And why is thy countenance fallen?"*

Cain did not give his first fruits as God instructed. He did not do his best. We should always try to do our best. God considers an honest try perfect.

Genesis 4:7. *"If thou dost well, shalt thou not be accepted? And if thou dost not well, sin lieth at the door. And unto thee shall be His desire, and thou shall rule over him."*

This is truly "Fatherly" advice.

Genesis 4:8. *"And Cain talked with Abel his brother: and it came to pass, when they were in the field, that Cain rose up against his brother and slew him."*

The manuscripts say that Cain "asked" Abel to go into the field. This makes the murder of Abel premeditated, and that is "murder one" in God's book. It is lucky for Cain that the law and its punishment for murder had not yet been given to Moses.

Genesis 4:9. *"And the Lord said unto Cain, where is Abel thy brother? And he said, I know not; Am I my brother's keeper?"*

"I know not," is a lie. Cain's father is a liar – "he is the father of it" (John 8:44). Cain is pure evil; he even smarts off to God. The old apple does not fall too far from this tree.

Genesis 4:10. *"And He said, "What hast thou done?" the voice of thy brothers blood crieth unto me from the ground."*

God is fully aware of what Cain has done. God did not ask Cain's father any questions. Why is He bothering with Cain? As you continue reading, it becomes apparent that God does it for our benefit.

Genesis 4:11. *"And now thou art cursed from the earth, which has opened her mouth to receive thy brother's blood from thy hand."*

This is why Kenites, (children of Cain) cannot farm. The earth has been "cursed" to them. That being said all that any of God's children, Kenites or otherwise, have to do is accept Christ as their savior per John 3:16 and they are saved.

Genesis 4:12. *"When thou tillest the ground, it shall not henceforth yield to thee her strength; a fugitive and a vagabond shalt thou be in the earth."*

Remember, Cain is a farmer. It is his livelihood, and now it is gone. What will Cain do? We will see that he is going to build cities and get married. Think about this. Who is Cain going to marry? Someone from the 6th day creation. And who is Cain going to build cities for? - All God's children, created on the sixth day, some 2,000 years before Adam and Eve.

Genesis 4:13. *"And Cain said unto the Lord, my punishment is more than I can bare."*

It could have been worse, as indicated in Deuteronomy 19:11-12, Deuteronomy 21:22-23 and Exodus 21:12-14. Yes, the death penalty is biblical. Why would God in these verses instruct us to execute murderers and rapists? The answer is in Deuteronomy 19:11-13.

"So it may go well with you."

In other words, if you dispatch a murderer or a child rapist, they will never have a chance to do it again. Not only that, other would-be criminals will see the repercussions for this action and think very hard about doing the same thing. Let's face it – most criminals are cowards. God created mankind, and He knows what works. He said.

"Do this and these things 'will cease to happen'." And

"Send them to me."

This makes sense. With our all-knowing Father, they won't have need of a slick lawyer. God knows all the facts. Remember, there are two deaths; execution is just the flesh death. Maybe they will get it together in the millennium. Remember what Christ said, "I do not change one jot or title of the law." Some of mankind always think they know best. Couple this with the fact that most do not read the Bible, and you have the debacle that is our justice system of today.

Genesis 4:14. *"Behold, thou hast driven me out this day from the face of the earth; and from thy face I shall be hid; and I shall be a fugitive and a vagabond in the earth; and it shall come to pass, that everyone that findeth me shall slay me."*

Cain has the mark of the beast. It is not anywhere on his body. It is an "evil spirit" within him. Christians are able to discern evil spirits. Remember, Cain's father is the devil, documentation (John 8:44). Remember the first prophesy of the Bible in which God put "hatred" between Eve and her children the children of light and satan's children the Kenites. It is for this reason there will never be total peace on earth in this age until the end. And as you will discover this is the time to fear most.

Genesis 4:15. *"And the Lord said unto him, 'Therefore whosoever slayeth Cain, vengeance shall be taken on him seven fold. And the Lord set a mark upon Cain, lest any finding him should kill him."*

There's that mark. Cain is needed to carry out the negative part of God's plan. Every positive needs a negative. He is the son of the devil. (Genesis 3:16) There was a "conception" in the Garden. Cain is not just the son of the devil – he is the father of the Kenites. They are born into this flesh age through Cain's genealogy because of their actions in the first earth age. They stood with satan instead of God in the rebellion. If you teach this truth you are going to be two things for sure – one, unpopular with a lot of people and two, pleasing in God's eyes. When you know this truth and bring it forward to today, it goes a long way to explaining the events unfolding in the world at this time. In these end times satan is allowed to bring forth his best (worst) as God is allowed to bring forth the best He has. Satan's efforts in this department have been building for decades, in my opinion. Could this be why in the 50's, 60's, and partly the 70's, kids could go all day without reporting to their parents as opposed to today where you can't let go of your child's hand in a public place?

Genesis 4:16. *"And Cain went from the presence of the Lord, and dwelt in the land of Nod."*

"Nod" = "wandering or the land of nomads." Its location is near Mongolia of today.

Genesis 4:17. *"And Cain knew his wife; and she conceived, and bare Enoch: and he builded a city' and called the name of the city' after the name of his son' Enoch."*

What's this? Cain married. Who? Cain's wife is the offspring of the sixth day creation. Cain built a city for whom? Again, the sixth day of creation. There are probably millions of people upon the earth by this time. Remember, God cursed the ground to Cain, so he cannot farm, nor can his offspring. They are builders of cities.

There you have it, the truth, chapter by chapter and verse by verse. If you decide to read further on your own, be aware that the rest of this chapter and chapter five gives the blood line of Adam up to Noah. It is Adam's genealogy, his blood line, and Noah is in it. We will pick up with Noah and the flood in the next chapter. If you read chapter five of Genesis, note that Cain's name does not appear anywhere in Adam's genealogy. Why? He is not Adam's son. Yes, I know, Abel's name does not appear either. This is because Abel was murdered before he had children, his legacy dying with him. Cain did have children. The fact that Cain's name does not appear in Eth-Ha-Adams, The Adams genealogy is more proof that Cain's father is the devil.

Let's review what we have read. We have seen the creation of this earth age and all the inhabitants in it. We have discovered that Adam and Eve were not the first humans to inhabit this earth in this age and that there were thousands upon thousands of people before them. We've learned that God was very pleased with His creation, all of it, up until satan got to Eve. We now know that Cain's offspring are the Kenites. They represent the negative part of God's plan, are troublemakers that bear watching, and still exist today. No, they weren't destroyed in Noah's flood. Noah was instructed to take "two of every flesh" into the ark. The Kenites were and are flesh today. In the next chapter, we will bring "fact" to the "myths" that cloud the truth concerning the "real reason" for Noah's flood.

CHAPTER 4

NOAH'S FLOOD AND THE FALLEN ANGELS

Genesis 5:32. *"And Noah was 500 years Old; And Noah begat "Shem, Ham, and Japheth."*

These are Noah's sons. They, their wives, Noah's wife, and two of every flesh will accompany Noah on the ark only 100 years after the writing of this verse. It is always important to fix a time frame when reading God's word. We are only 100 years from the flood. The year is 2,448 B.C., only 726 years after the death of Adam. There are no doubt millions of people on the earth at this time. Because satan was allowed to "walk" the earth, and because mankind has free will, evil is abounding. In fact, it is the order of the day. Let's move on to Chapter 6:1 in this Book of Genesis and let Our Father's word describe the key event that caused Him to bring about "The Great Flood" of Noah's time. As was the case in the Garden of Eden, it is doubtful you have been taught the truth about this event. Let us continue our search for the truth. The truth will ultimately allow us to positively identify the antichrist and his method of operation.

Genesis 6:1. *"And it came to pass, when men began to multiply on the face of the earth and daughters were born to them."*

God, on the sixth day, said, *"replenish"* the earth. And so they are. These daughters (women) born of mankind, are going to be the target of the fallen angels. The fallen angels saw these beautiful mortal women and would marry them. Your documentation is found in Jude Chapter 1. Jude is the brother of Jesus Christ. Read the first eleven verses. Jude is talking about the fallen angels.

Genesis 6:2. *"That the "sons of God"* (fallen angels) *saw the daughters of men that they were fair; and they took them wives of all which they choose."*

The "Sons of God" are the fallen angels, those of God's children, "angelic beings," who took up with satan back at the end of the first earth age, at the katabole', (satan's rebellion). These angelic beings refused to be born in flesh, in this age, innocent, with no recollection of that first age, to prove if they will love God or satan. This is the first mention of these evil angels in God's word, however, we will see they are mentioned throughout the Bible. These angels are also called "sons of God" because it is only by a Divine, specific and direct act of creation (by God) that any being can be called "a son of God." In the first earth age, we were all called "sons of God," because in that age, we were created (by God), not born (of woman).

An example of this can be read in Job 38:7. The setting for this verse is back in the first earth age, sometime before satan's rebellion. Verse 38 reads.

"When the morning stars sang together, and all the sons of God shouted for joy."

'Morning stars' is one of God's pet names for us back in the first age. *"All The* sons *of God."* "All," indicates all of Our Father's creation and that we, those who obeyed God and chose to be born in flesh, were there, not just the fallen angels. Additional documentation is found in Luke 3:38. This verse gives us Jesus Christ's genealogy. As has been documented earlier; Christ's blood line began with Adam. 'Eth Ha Adam, The man Adam and Eve. Notice that Adam is called a "son of God" in this verse, unlike his offspring, Seth, Enos, and the others mentioned all the way to Christ, who are called "sons of man." Why? Again, they were born of woman. Adam was created from clay "directly" by God and had no mother. Therefore, even though he was created in this second earth age into flesh, he is called "a son of God." He is the first man of the Adamic race.

The fallen angels are mentioned in the New Testament in the book of Jude. Jude, in the first verse, states that he is the brother of James who is the brother of Christ. That Christ had siblings is documented in Mark 6:3.

"Is not this the carpenter, the son of Mary, the brother of James, and Joses, and of Juda (Jude), *and Simon? And are not His sisters here with us?"*

Christ had sisters as well. Jude obviously knew Christ very well, so his account of these evil angels is credible. Quoting from Jude 6:4.

"For there are certain men (ish') *crept in unawares, who were before of Old ordained to this condemnation, ungodly men* (the fallen angels), *turning the grace of our God into lasciviousness, and denying the only Lord God, and our Lord, Jesus Christ."*

Verse 5. *"I will therefore put you in remembrance, though you once knew this, How that the Lord, having saved the people out of the land of Egypt, afterward destroyed them that believed not* (with the flood)."

Verse 6. *"And the angels which kept not their first estate* (heaven, that dimension), *He hath reserved in everlasting chains under darkness unto the judgment of the great day"* (Talking about judgment day). "One day to God is as 1000 years to man."

Verse 7. *"Even as Sodom and Gomorrah, and the cities about them, in like manner giving themselves over to fornication, and going after strange flesh* (homosexuality), *are set forth for an example, suffering the vengeance of eternal fire."*

The fallen angels, like satan, have already been judged and will be destroyed. The fallen angels (there are 7,000) will meet their demise at the end of this earth age (Revelation 11:13), and satan, not until the end of the millennium. These verses tell us that these Godless perverts have been in Sodom and Gomorrah. Today they are in heaven, locked in chains and held by Michael the archangel. The bad news is that they are coming back. Soon. Never forget this information. The Apostle Matthew documents this prophesy in Matthew 24:37.

"But as the days of Noah were, so shall also the coming of the son of man (Christ) *be."*

In plain English; as things were in Noah's time so they shall be again, at the time just before Jesus Christ returns. You will realize as you read further the times we are living in now are undeniably similar to the last days prior to the flood. Still more documentation can be found in Revelation 12:7-9. The book of Revelation, written by John the apostle around 96 A.D., in any language you may interpret it, means "to reveal" or "make known." The following events are in the not too distant future.

"And there was war in heaven; Michael and His angels fought against the dragon and his angels,"

Verse 8. *"And prevailed not, neither was there place found anymore in heaven."* (Time to go).

Verse 9. *"And the great dragon was cast out, that Old serpent, called the devil and satan, which deceiveth the whole world: He was cast out unto the earth, and his angels were cast out with him."*

Verse 9. Gives us a few of the names that satan is called by and documents that the "serpent" in the Garden of Eden was, in fact, satan. Michael is going to "cast" satan (who when this action takes place becomes the antichrist) out of heaven. This is one reason why I say that satan (the antichrist) will not be born of woman in flesh. He and the fallen angels will be "cast," which translated means "thrown out" of heaven, "that dimension." The term "thrown out" carries with it the connotation of "violently." They will not be born "innocent babes" as we were. Make no mistake, the antichrist is not alive on this earth at this time growing older waiting for the right time to make his move. He is in heaven causing as much turmoil as he possibly can.

Do not read over the statement *"Which deceiveth the whole world,"* in verse 9 previous. You are being warned. Satan will be so convincing that everyone, with the exception of those who know the truth, this very truth we are studying, will be deceived.

You do not want to be worshiping satan, as the "antichrist," when the true Christ returns. "Anti" in the Greek language means "instead of." Satan as antichrist will return first, that's next, at the sixth trumpet. Christ will not return until the seventh trumpet and not until satan has had his time as the antichrist to deceive as many as he can. Again, you do not want to be worshiping the devil when The Lord returns. The fallen angels, like antichrist (satan), will not be ugly, brute beasts (Revelation 9:7). The subject of Chapter 9 is the fallen angels.

Verse 7. "And on their heads were as it were crowns like gold, and their faces were as the faces of men."

The book of Revelation is full of symbolism. Without a little help from the manuscripts it would be impossible to understand, so let's go ahead and break this verse down. *"*Crowns like gold*"* is an idiom meaning "they will look regal, like royalty, very impressive." And note that they had the faces of men: "They look like 'mortal men' (Adam), but they are "supernatural men" (ish'). They, like satan, should look pretty normal to us, because our other (angelic) bodies are made of a better substance, but they are not all that different looking. The wise in Our Father's word should be able to spot these frauds. Revelation 9:8 makes this clear.

"And they had the hair as the hair of women, and their teeth were as the teeth of lions."

Once again, we are dealing with symbolism in the phrase *"hair as the hair of a woman."* This is telling us that these beings will appear and act "gentle" and "soft spoken," but looks can be deceiving, *"the teeth of lions."* Although they look gentle, they will be speaking lies designed to shred and tear apart a soul. Lies that if you believe, can even kill your soul, and that's the second death. This will be the ultimate deception and why Christ said in Matthew 10:28.

"And fear not them which kill the (your) *body, but are not able to kill the soul: but rather fear him that is able to destroy both soul and body to hell."*

These angels will be helping satan with his plan of deception as antichrist. Picking back up in the book of Revelation 9:9.

"And they had breastplates, as it were breastplates of iron; and the sound of their wings was as the sound of chariots of many horses running into battle."

The fallen angels, having mass, will need vehicles. This description is the best St. John could do some 2,000 years ago. "Chariot" in the Hebrew means "To ride."

Verse 10. *"And they (the fallen angels) had tails like unto scorpions, and there were stings in their tails: and their power was to hurt men five months."*

The word *"hurt"* used here is "adikeo'" in the Greek language. Its meaning is to "do wrong" (morally). In this case the fallen angels will be lying, saying "see Christ has returned." The *Bible* states, and I will document later, that satan as antichrist will be able to perform miracles in the site of everyone alive on this earth. To best explain the above verse we will need to back up to Revelation 9:5. The subject of this verse is the fallen angels.

"And to them (the fallen angels) *it was given that they should not kill them* (us), *but that they* (us) *should be tormented five months: and their torment was as the torment of a scorpion, when it striketh a man."*

This verse not only contains, but epitomizes, the proverbial scenario of good news, bad news. First, the good news. This is the best news since salvation itself. Christ, in Mark 13:20, shortened the time of the tribulation from seven years to just five months. However, God's word tells us that this will be long enough to wear down even the most devoted if they do not have the truth sealed in their brain. We will be covering Mark Chapter 13 in an upcoming chapter. But for now, this fifth verse of Revelation Chapter 9 also tells us how the fallen angel will deceive the unlearned in God's word.

First the word "torment" is commonly connected with "demons." To understand their "torment" or better stated, their method of operation, you must understand how a scorpion eats. A scorpion has no stomach. Therefore it must use its victim as a stomach. It does this by striking the victim with its tail and injecting a poison that paralyzes the victim, rendering it unable to move. The scorpion then turns the helpless victim toward its mouth, where concealed inside are its needle-sharp fangs. Grasping the prey with its crablike pinchers, the scorpion places the victim in its mouth, injecting it with venom that turns the victim's skeletal structure, including the backbone, to mush. The victim's insides become a meal while the surrounding skin acts as the scorpion's stomach. This is how the fallen angels and satan will operate. They will use their "venomous lies," "tails" or "tall tales" better said, to turn the backbones of their unlearned, denominationally dumbed-down victims to mush, metaphorically speaking, causing them to worship satan as antichrist. The fallen angels have been here on this earth before, and it is written that they are going to return. It is written, and it will happen exactly as it is written. Never forget that the real battle with Antichrist will be a spiritual not a physical battle. This is why in Ephesians 6:11-17 instructs us to put on the Gospel armor.

Before we move on and read for ourselves just what was going on that angered God so much that He brought about the Great Flood, let's turn to the New Testament and let Paul, the author of most of it, give documentation that these evil angels are going to return. Paul, a reformed persecutor of Christians, did not start his ministry until around 35 years after our Lord was crucified. There are some critics who try to discredit Paul by saying that he never even met Jesus Christ. They obviously have not done their homework as his meeting with our Lord is well documented in Acts 9:1-9 on the road to Damascus. Not only that, but God Almighty Himself says in Acts 9:15 that Paul is "His chosen vessel" in whom He (God) is well pleased. If that is not sufficient, Peter, in 2 Peter 3:15-16, acknowledges Paul's God-given wisdom. With that said, let's read what Paul has to say about the fallen angels in 1 Corinthians 11:10.

"For this cause ought the woman to have power (Christ/truth) *over her head because of the angels."*

'Power' here is Christ, and the angels are the fallen angels. Why does Paul give this warning? They are coming back. And they will be looking for women – women who do not know the truth. Let's get back to the Book of Genesis and continue reading about the flood.

Genesis 6:3. *"And the Lord said, my spirit shall not always strive with man, for that he also is flesh yet his days shall be a hundred and twenty years."*

The man spoken of specifically here is Eth-Ha'-Adam, the man, Eve's husband. He has 120 years left, but this verse is not just for him. Let's use the information that God has given us to affix a time frame. God is telling us, the reader, that Adam has exactly 120 years to live. Adam died in the year 3,074 B.C., when he was 930 years old. So we know Adam, at this time, is 810 years old. Therefore, the year of this verse is 3,194 B.C. This is 3,194 years before Christ will be born, and only 846 years before the flood.

Genesis 6:4. *"There were giants on the earth in those days; and also after that, when the "sons of God"* (the fallen angels) *came unto* (in) *the daughters of men and they bare children to them, the same became mighty men which were of Old, men of renown."*

There is so much being said in this verse that unless you have a better then good understanding of the Bible, you will never be able to fully figure it out. So, let's break it down and shine the light of truth on it. First, the word "unto" is incorrect. The word in the manuscripts is "bow,'" which means "in." Reread this verse correctly and you can see that, like satan, the fallen angels are able to impregnate mortal women. The way that it was, is the way that it is written. That is that. "The sons of God," the fallen angels, were on this earth. They did father children, and they are coming back. This is satan's second attempt to pollute the Adamic line, the first being with Eve in the Garden. This is "Eth-ha-adams" line, through which Christ was to come. If he is able to prevent the birth of the Savior, satan believes he can avoid his own doom.

The result of angelic beings (the fallen angels) mating with flesh women were "giants." These giants were mighty men sometimes called "gibbor." Their fathers are the fallen angels, who were also at times called "Ne-phil'-im" from the prime root "naphal," which means 'to fall'. Their reputation was well known, and they were greatly feared. The destruction of these gibbor was necessary for the preservation of the human race. This is the sole reason for the flood of Noah's time." As it was in the time of Noah, so shall it be in these end days." Matthew 24:37.

Probably the most renown of these giants was "Goliath," the same giant that David slew. 1 Samuel Chapter 17 gives us some idea as to the size and strength of one of these abnormal beings. Goliath was approximately 13 feet tall. The combined weight of his armor was 237 pounds not including his spear, which weighed 36 pounds, and measured 23 feet in length. Another "giant" of lesser fame was named "Og" (Deuteronomy 3:11). This giant was the King of Bashan whose bed was 18' long, 8'4" wide and made of iron, not wood. Note in this verse the words "and after that." The fact that there was another influx or more of the fallen angels after the flood is documented in Numbers 13:33 and Deuteronomy 10-11. it is apparent that these angels were able to escape the flood waters. But how? Keep reading.

Genesis 6:5. *"And God saw that the wickedness of man was great in the earth, and that every imagination of the thoughts of his heart was only evil continually."*

If man (Adam/mankind) was not actually acting wickedly, he was thinking about it. God is fed up. It is looking a lot like today. Noah's time was a time of unimaginable lawlessness and perversion. God would no longer tolerate the molestation, sacrificing, and murdering of children at the hands of the fallen angels and their spawn. For similarities you need only to look at the world today.

Genesis 6:6. *"And it repented the Lord that he had made man on the earth, and it grieved him at his heart."*

If you have ever wondered if God has feelings, here is your proof. "Repented" means "to hurt." It broke God's heart that man was capable of such atrocities. "Grieved" as it is used here means "angered," as to the point of tears. God was ticked! He is seriously considering destroying the whole smash. He has done it before, and he is about to do it again. It is looking like the end of the second earth age is about to take place ahead of schedule.

Genesis 6:7. *"And the Lord said, "I will destroy man whom I have created from the face of the earth; both man, and beast, and the creeping thing, and the fouls of the air; for it repenteth me that I have made him."*

Satan's attempt to destroy Christ's bloodline has been very successful. Everyone had mixed with the fallen angels, the "naphalium" with only one exception, Noah and his family.

Genesis 6:8. *"But Noah found grace in the eyes of the Lord."*

Noah and his family had not mixed with the fallen angels. They had a perfect pedigree. Noah and his family will continue the line through which Christ would come.

Genesis 6:9. *"These are the generations of Noah: Noah was a just man and perfect in his generations and Noah walked with God."*

Generations = pedigree or family history. Noah's family has had nothing to do with the fallen angels or their offspring. We can only imagine how tough things must have been for them. Things may get a little rough for those of us who do not participate in satan's deception at the end of this world age. But no worries, God takes care of His own.

Genesis 6:10. *"And Noah* (had) *begat three sons, Shem, Ham, Japheth."*

The year is now 2,448 B.C., just 100 years before the flood and only a short 4,496 ago.

Genesis 6:11. *"The earth also was corrupt before God, and the earth was filled with violence."*

Never forget, as it was in Noah's time, so it will be again.

Genesis 6:12. *"And God looked up from the earth, and behold, it was corrupt; for all flesh had corrupted His* (God's) *way upon the earth."*

This is talking about unnatural acts of the flesh, homosexuality as well as the raping of children. It is well known what was going on in "Sodom and Gomorrah" during the time of Noah. The fallen angels were orchestrating the perversion in these cities. If you are at all curious as to how Our Father feels about "the matter," read Leviticus 20:13 and Deuteronomy 22:5. When reading Deuteronomy 22:5, keep in mind that men wore skirts at that time, so the subject is not clothes. "All flesh" is with the exception of Noah's family. Noah's wife, his three sons and their wives. They did not mix with the fallen angels. Remember, God is preserving the line through which Christ would come.

Genesis 6:13. **"***And God said to Noah, "the end of all flesh has come before me; for the earth is filled with violence through them* (the fallen angels and the gibbor); *and behold, I will destroy them with the earth."*

Notice the words "through them." God is referring to the fallen angels and their offspring. They have created all the confusion. In Genesis 6:14-18), God instructs Noah to build an ark and gives him instructions on how it is to be built.

Genesis 6:19. *"And of every living thing of all flesh, two of every sort shalt thou bring into the ark, to keep them alive with thee; they shall be male and female."*

"Two of every flesh," not just the animals. This command from on High no doubt includes two Kenites. Every positive needs a negative.

Genesis 7:5. *"And Noah did according unto all that the Lord commanded Him."*

Noah is a good and faithful servant.

Genesis 7:6. *"And Noah was six hundred years Old when the flood waters were upon the earth."*

The flood has not begun yet, but Noah's age is an important benchmark. Keep it in mind.

Genesis 7:7. *"And Noah went in, and his sons and his wife and his sons wives with him, into the ark, because of the waters of the flood."*

It is hard to imagine the amount of faith Noah possessed to not only construct the ark but to enter into it. No doubt Noah has had all kinds of harassment. God tells us that man's behavior was like that of today's, so I would imagine that more than one attempt to burn the ark was made. I would not want to have been in their shoes when God handled the threat. Our Father commanded that the ark be built, therefore it was going to get built. As Paul said in Romans 8:31.

"If God be for us, who can be against us?"

Genesis 7:8. *"Of clean beasts, and of beasts that are not clean, and of fouls, and of everything that creepeth upon the earth."*

Genesis 7:9. *"There went in two and two unto Noah into the ark, the male and the female, as God had command Noah."*

This actually happened. One can only imagine the look on the faces of the doomed bystanders. There is no way we can know if Noah or members of his family had told the mass of onlookers the plan, but whether they did or did not, this event must have gotten everyone's attention. The flood is only seven days away now. The year is 2348 BC.

Genesis 7:10. *"And it came to pass after seven days, that the waters of the flood were upon the earth."*

Noah, his family, and the other occupants of the ark are safely tucked away on-board. Meanwhile outside, the thick dark, ominous clouds that had been gathering for days begin to let loose. Imagine the faces of the hecklers, their heads and palms turned skyward, eyes wide open, staring with the glazed look of someone about to be hit by a bus. Suddenly, they realize that from below, the ground waters are reaching for their ankles. Panicked, they push and shove at the ark and one another. The party is over. This day, they will meet their maker.

Although the events taking place in this verse happened thousands of years ago, there is a lesson that applies to us today. The Bible states that there is another flood coming at the end of this earth age. It is not a flood as you may think, but rather a "flood of lies" from antichrist's (satan's) mouth, documentation Revelation 12:15.

"And the serpent (satan as antichrist) *cast out of his mouth water* (lies) *as a flood after the woman* (religions), *that he might cause her* (the church and all the dumbed-down sheep/members) *to be carried away* (deceived) *of the flood."*

Again, we are talking about a flood of lies from satan's mouth. Satan is going to use a religious platform as his M.O. (method of operation). This is the second beast of Revelation, the first beast being a one-world government system. Socialism. See anything going on like that today? Satan, the devil, that old serpent is "a liar and the father of lying." The time frame of this verse is at the very end of this earth age, during antichrist's five-month tribulation. Never forget this, satan is the antichrist. But if you want to know exactly how he operates step by step, you will have to keep reading. "Anti" in the Greek language means "instead of." Satan will be claiming to be Christ, and all the while, lies will be cascading out from his mouth. When the flood of lies begins this time, you want to be in the "ark" of "truth" with any "gaps" having been pitched (plugged) with knowledge in God's word, describes in Daniel 11:24.

"He (the antichrist) *shall enter peaceably even upon the fattest places of the province...He shall scatter among them the prey and the spoil and the riches."*

Because the antichrist comes in "peacefully" and "prosperously," be prepared to fend off the hecklers knocking at the door of your ark. Those who are deceived will think you are an atheist. They believe Jesus Christ has "returned." As you let this information settle, realize there is so much more you need to know about this subject and I promise you I will get there but for now let's continue on our journey.

Genesis 7:11. *"In the six hundredth year of Noah's life, in the second month, the seventeenth day of the month, the same day were all the fountains of the great deep broken up, and the windows of heaven were opened."*

Noah is 600 years old. It is February 17, 2,348 B.C., and the flood starts. The flood was from below (ground waters rising), as well as from above.

Genesis 7:12: *"And the rain was upon the earth forty days and forty nights."*

It rains 40 days and 40 nights. Forty in biblical numerics means "probation." The gestation period of a human fetus is not nine months. It is actually 40 weeks.

Genesis 7:13-14. Noah loads the ark.

Genesis 7:15. *"And they went in unto Noah into the ark, two and two of all flesh, where in is the breath of life."*

"Breath of life" as it is used here in the Hebrew language is "ruach" which means, "spirit."

Let's skip down to
Genesis 7:24. *"And the waters prevailed upon the earth a hundred and fifty days."*

One hundred and fifty days = five months. The number five in biblical numerics means "grace." Five months is the same amount of time as the tribulation of antichrist in the end days. The "great tribulation" spoken of by Daniel the prophet was a seven-year period, shortened by Christ Himself to five months in Mark 13:20 below.

"And except that the Lord had shortened those days, no flesh should be saved: but for the Elects' sake, whom He hath chosen, He hath shortened the days."

Thank God for this. Revelation 9:5 tells us the tribulation has been shortened to "5 months."

Noah and those on the ark have been floating around for five months now. That is a long time, but no doubt their daily chores are keeping them occupied. Do not forget that the Kenites are on board as well, and they are troublemakers, so there may be some strife at times. But Noah and his sons can handle it. The period of time on the ark was still the time of the daily sacrifice, twice daily, as a matter of fact. We know that this law was being observed on the ark, because God told Noah back in verse two of this chapter to take seven each of the clean animals for sacrifice, plus a male and female in addition to those to be for sacrifice. After sacrifice, the animals could be eaten by those aboard the ark. That is undoubtedly how Noah and the others ate. Skipping down to Genesis 8:1 we read,

"And God remembered Noah and every living thing, and all the cattle that was with him on the ark: God made a wind to pass over the earth, and the waters were assuaged." (abated).

God is taking care of those in the ark for they are the ones who are going to "replenish" the earth yet again in this flesh age. God will look after those who do not worship the antichrist with the same loving care during the five months of the tribulation. It is written. It will happen.

Genesis 8:2. *"The fountains also of the deep and the windows of heaven were stopped, and the rain from heaven restrained."*

Genesis 8:3. *"And the waters returned from off the earth continually: and after the hundred and fifty days the waters were abated."*

Five months into the flood and the waters are pulling back.

Genesis 8:4. *"And the ark rested in the seventh month, on the seventeenth day of the month, upon the mountains of Ararat."*

"Ararat" means "high ground." The ark comes to rest on high ground. It is July 17, 2,348 B.C. They went into the ark on February 17, 2,348, exactly five months previous.

Genesis 8:7. *"And he sent forth a raven, which went forth to and fro, until the waters were dried up from off the earth."*

Noah sent forth a raven. It did not come back, and this is no surprise. After all, a raven is a scavenger. No doubt this bird found plenty to eat.

Genesis 8:8. *"And he sent forth a dove from him, to see if the waters were abated from off the face of the ground."*

A dove represents the Holy Spirit. Eight in biblical numerics = "new beginnings." And so it was.

Genesis 8:9. *"But the dove found no rest for the sole of her foot, and she returned unto him in the ark."* It is not time yet.

Genesis 8:11. *"And the dove came in to him in the evening; and lo, in her mouth was an olive leaf plucked off: so Noah knew the waters were abated from off the earth."*

An olive tree takes years to grow; for that reason it is most often planted as a shoot. Noah and his crew have been in the ark less than a year, and the waters are for the most part gone. Noah's flood did not destroy the earth and everything in it, as most are led to believe. The katabole,' the flood that ended the first earth age did so many years before this flood. Let this give you some perspective regarding time sequences in the Bible.

Genesis 8:12. *"And he (Noah) stayed yet another seven days; and sent forth the dove; which returned not again unto him anymore."*

Seven in biblical numerics = "spiritual completeness." Numbers and their meanings are important to God. Noah tries once again. What faith this one man must have had.

Genesis 8:13. *"And it came to pass in the six hundredth and first year, in the first month, the first day of the month, the waters were dried up from off the earth: And Noah removed the covering of the ark, and looked and, behold, the face of the ground was dry."*

Noah is now 601 years old. Noah's age increases by one year, and the calendar decreases by one year. Remember, it is B.C., or "before Christ." God has given us two ways to measure the length of the flood, Noah's age and the year. Two in biblical numerics =

"witness," so, there can be no doubt and yet there are those who do not understand. Many still believe this flood destroyed this earth. This is why I say a good foundation in Our Father's word is important.

Genesis 8:14. *"And in the second month, on the seventh and twentieth day of the month, was the earth dried."*

This is February 20, 2,347 B.C., exactly one solar year from the floods beginning. Remember, we are children of the light. Moons or months vary, but the sun is always constant. All prophecy given to those who love Our Father is always in days. All prophecy given directed at satan and his ilk is given in months. Skipping to Genesis 8:22, we read,

"While the earth remaineth, seed time harvest, and cold and heat, and summer and winter, and day and night, shall not cease."

Note the word "shall." God is letting us know, in no uncertain terms, that He is in control. God in this verse gives us (4) examples of climate i.e. "Cold and heat," "summer and winter," etc. The #4 in biblical numerics always has to do with the earth as it does in this verse. That you see God is in control should explain His opinion on global warming. This earth will make it to the end of this age just fine. It is written, it will be. Everyone must however make up their own minds. Myself, I believe it is just another way of man trying to get control over his fellow man. You may ask, why is this wrong? The first beast spoken of in Revelation (there are two) is "a one-world governmental system," Socialism. The less you depend on government, and the more "self-sufficient" that you are, the easier it will be to ride out the tribulation.

The first beast, "one-world government," receives a "deadly wound." The second beast of Revelation is "religious." Satan (antichrist), when he returns to this earth claiming to be Christ, will use his "one-world religious system" to heal the "deadly wound" and therefore deceive "the whole world." Anytime you hear "global" this or "global" that, you need to pay attention. The end of this age could take place until these are possible. They are not only possible today, but the first beast is growing rapidly.

Genesis 8:13. *"I do set my bow in the cloud, and it shall be for a token of the covenant between me and the earth."*

The "bow" in the cloud mentioned here is the "rainbow." This colorful bow will always be a sign of the covenant (promise) that God will never bring about another flood on the earth, Noah's flood being the second. Remember, the next flood, the flood of these end times, will be a "flood of lies" from out of antichrist's (satan's) mouth. God never breaks a promise. Never!

Noah, his family and two of every flesh, set forth to "replenish" the earth yet again. This is the second time the earth has been replenished in this the second earth age, the flesh age (Genesis 1:28). The giants and all those who mixed with the fallen angels are dead. The fallen angels, however, have managed to escape. How do we know? The Bible documents that there were other influxes after the flood in Numbers 13:33 and Deuteronomy 2:10. Matthew 24:36-39 tells us that they are coming back. How? Just some food for thought as we leave this chapter. "The landing strip is in Peru." Read chapter one in the book of Ezekiel with your spiritual eyes open and Remember, when it comes to the end of this age, Our Father has told us all things. FYI, I intend to explain the first chapter of Ezekiel later in this book.

CHAPTER 5

PROPHESY AND PROMISES

Christ speaking, in Mark 13:23: *"But take you heed: behold I have foretold you all things."*

God, Our Father, is always fair. He promises that He will do nothing without telling us first. How? Through the prophets, as stated in Amos 3:7.

"Surely the Lord will do nothing, but (unless) He revealith His secret unto His servants the prophets."

The time of this prophesy is 688 B.C. This is just one of God's many promises. A witness to this promise can be found in the book of Isaiah. Isaiah prophesied from 649 to 588 B.C. and lived to be about 83 years old. Isaiah 42:9 depicts the following.

"Behold the former things have come to pass, and New things I do declare; before they spring forth I tell you."

Forewarned is forearmed. This is good advice as there is a fight coming, very soon. It is quite likely that if you are reading this, you will be alive to experience the fight. After having read the last two chapters of this book it is likely you may be a little apprehensive about the coming of the end of this earth age. That is just human nature. Most of us, however, pretty much only fear what we do not know. When we are warned of what is coming, our survival instincts kick in and the brave find a way around, over, under and even through the situation. An added bonus is knowing exactly how long that situation will last and if it has a definite ending at all.

Remember the fight that is coming is a spiritual battle. Not a physical fight.

It is for these reasons, knowing Our Father's prophesies and promises is now, more than ever, so very important. Our Father never lies, and He always keeps His promises. All we have to do is claim them, and to do that you have to know what they are. That is exactly what we are going to do in this chapter.

Reading prophesies in the Bible is like reading tomorrow's newspaper. From the Major Prophets Isaiah, Jeremiah and Ezekiel, through the Minor Prophets. Minor not due to content, but because these twelve prophets reports were short, as were the years that they prophesied. All throughout the Old and New Testament, Our Father tells us in advance about the events that must take place in this, the second earth age. Would anyone listen? The fact is that the vast majority of the world will not, as Jeremiah 6:17 says.

"Also I set watchmen over you, saying, Hearken (listen) to the trumpets (warnings) but they said, we will not hearken."

I made the statement that God has left nothing out, so I know what you are thinking: What about the end of the world? No one can know the day or the hour. Here is how the documentation appears in Mark 13:32.

"But of that day and that hour knoweth no man, no, not the angels which are in heaven, neither the Son, but the Father only."

First the manuscripts say that no man can know the "instant." This correction may seem trivial, but is important in keeping with the Bible's accuracy. Verses like this one and many others are why I say reading the Bible with understanding is so interesting. It has been called the greatest story ever told, and I agree. Look at Hollywood today – they are making and remaking movies based on biblical stories left and right.

But getting back to the previous verse, this statement is true today. It was certainly true when Christ said it some 2,000 years ago. However, by reading the *Bible* carefully, one can know the exact "hour" of the end of this earth age. That is right. It is not a sin or a secret. It can be known, and even more, this is information that Our Father wants us to know. God wants those who love Him enough to take the time to search, to discover it. He told us in Mark 13:23 that He has told us everything when it comes to the end times. The answer to determining the exact hour lies in the Book of Revelation Chapter 11. Revelation, in any language you interpret it, means 'to reveal.' If you have ever been told that you do not need to read the book of Revelation think again. Revelation Ch. 1:3 tells the reader that, "you are blessed" if you read this book.

Let me set it up for you first. God's two witnesses is the subject of Chapter 11. You may have heard of them. They appear as event #3 on your "sequence of events chart." These witnesses will return in the end days, to prophesy against the antichrist during the five-month tribulation. God commands that no one dare touch these Prophets, however, satan and the fallen angels will not heed this warning. In the end days, these two witnesses from God will have been doing a lot of damage through their testimonies, thereby exposing satan's game plan. Toward the end of the tribulation period, satan and his fallen angels, drunk on prideful power and losing their grip on those deceived, now feel they have no choice but to kill these two ministers of God. Let us pick it up in Revelation 11:7.

"And when they (the two witnesses') shall have finished their testimony, the beast (satan/antichrist and his religious system) *that ascendeth out of the bottomless pit, shall make war against them, and shall overcome them, and kill them."*

This is a prophesy, and it will happen. This deliberate act is a no-no. God said,

"Touch not my Elect," and He meant it.

And in verse 8, God says, *"And their* (the two witnesses) *dead bodies shall lie in the street of the great city. This city spiritually called Sodom and Egypt, and it is where Our Lord was crucified."*

Borders have moved one way or the other over the centuries, and at one time or another, we can fix the location as Jerusalem. We know that Christ, our Lord, was most definitely crucified in Jerusalem. The word 'street' as it is used in this verse is 'plateia' in the original Greek manuscripts. It means a very wide and public place, most likely an arena. The bottom line is that the two witnesses will be killed in a very public place, which we read in Verse 9.

"And they of the people and kindreds and tongs and nations shall see their dead bodies (lie there) *three and one half days and shall not suffer their dead bodies to be put in graves."*

Satan, as antichrist, along with the fallen angels and many others who have been deceived, will not bury these bodies. Why not? Satan and his following are a very superstitious bunch, as one might expect. Certainly, satan and the fallen angels know that God is watching, and they remember when Christ was placed in the tomb. He got away. They do not want these two truth merchants to escape, so this time they are going to keep an eye on them. The above verse basically states that pretty much everyone will be able to see this event, most likely on television via satellite or the internet. God's word does document this in Psalms 37:34. The previous verses in Chapter 37 of Psalms have set the time as that of the very last days of this earth age. Psalms 37:34,

"When the wicked are cut off, thou shalt see it."

Continuing in Revelation Ch. 11, verse 10.

"And they that dwell on the earth shall rejoice over them (the

two witnesses), and make merry, and shall send gifts to one another; because these two prophets tormented them that dwelt on the earth."

These deviants have just murdered God's witnesses, probably Moses and Elisa, as they were the two who appeared on the mount of transfiguration (Matthew 17:3-4), but be that as it may, these murderers are celebrating and exchanging gifts. You need to think about the situation for a minute. All flesh on the earth at this time will think the antichrist and his evil angels are Christ and His angels returned. Satan and his fallen angels know exactly what is going on here, but to the rest of those on earth who are deceived, we that know the truth will certainly be looked upon as atheists and no doubt deeply hated by now. Think about it. Those who are deceived will believe with their whole hearts that this man is Jesus Christ and that he is standing right in front of them. Antichrist, who is pretending to be Christ will not lift a hand to hurt the Elect, however, those who are deceived will want to destroy us. Our father is always fair and always gives us "types" to sharpen our minds. You can see an example of this today In the Kenites "mantra" convert or die. This is when the good news for those of us not deceived comes, and the party ends for the others, as indicated in Revelation 11:11.

"And after three and one half days the Spirit of Life (ruach) from God entered into them (the two dead witnesses), *and they stood upon their feet; and great fear fell upon them which saw this."*

Imagine what must be going through the minds of those attending this party, not to mention those watching this take place via TV and the internet. Now that you have been given this revelation, I hope that you will be one of those watching. Watching, but not participating in the partying. The expression 'great fear' is one word in the manuscripts. It is "epipipto," and it means a ' paralyzing fear.' The partiers, those standing around in the arena, will be so shocked that they will literally wet themselves. Verse 12:

"And they heard a great voice from heaven saying unto them, come up hither, and they (God's witnesses) ascended up to heaven in a cloud; and their enemies beheld them."

They watched. Again, you do not want to be backing the wrong horse when this event comes down. The second coming of the true Jesus Christ is just seconds away. You now know directly from Our Father's word that when the two witnesses are killed in Jerusalem, there are only three and one half days (the same length of time our Lord was in the tomb) until Christ returns, this world age ends, and the millennium begins. A witness to this event is described by Paul in 1 Corinthians 15:51-52.

"In the blink of an eye, all that are alive on this earth are changed; into our celestial bodies.

Back to Revelation 11:13.

"And in the same hour (that the 2 witnesses' rise up) was there a great earthquake and a tenth part of the city fell and in the earthquake were slain (killed) of men seven thousand; and the remnant were affrightend, and gave glory to the God of heaven. Every knee shall bow."

Men mentioned here are supernatural men, not flesh men. The 7,000 killed at this time are the fallen angels. They are destroyed and will never be heard of again. Satan, however, still has some work to do at the end of the millennium (see your chart). The last part of the above verse is yet future and was prophesied by Isaiah 45:23 over 3,000 years ago. The Apostle Paul quotes it in the New Testament in Romans 14:11.

"As I live, saith the Lord, every knee shall bow to me, and every tongue shall confess to God."

This prophesy will be fulfilled, exactly as advertised. Let us pick it back up with Revelation 11:14 to finish.

"The second woe is past; and behold, the third woe cometh quickly."

The word 'quickly' used here is "tachu" in the Greek language. It means 'without delay,' so the event that follows in verse 15 happens immediately, without any delay. Let us see what happens next, in verse 15.

"And the seventh angel sounded (the trumpet), and there were great voices in heaven, saying, 'the kingdoms of this world (this world age) are become the kingdoms of the Lord and His Christ; and He shall reign forever and ever."

The moment being described here is the sounding of the seventh and last trumpet, heralding the return of Jesus Christ and the end of this, the second earth age. A quick review; satan returns as the antichrist at the sixth trumpet and the real Christ does not appear until the seventh and last trumpet. We now begin the millennium. Having read verse by verse, using God's word as documentation, it is as though you had been placed into a time machine, taken to the future, and shown exactly what will happen in the end days of this flesh age. That is how prophesy works. Never store this information too far back in your memory, as the time of the fulfillment of these verses is so very close. You are truly blessed and now know what 99 percent of the earth's inhabitants do not know. When the two witnesses are killed in Jerusalem, there are only three and one half days until the return of our savior Jesus Christ. Revelation 16:15 tells us.

"Behold, I come as a thief. Blessed is he that watcheth."

I in no way recommend waiting until the last days to get right with God, but armed with this knowledge you should not be caught off guard. This event, Christ's return, is mentioned on some 10,380 occasions throughout the Bible. Before this event takes place (Christ's return), the antichrist shall return. Remember, the purpose of this book is to expose the antichrist and his plan, thereby protecting your soul's immortality. Before we search God's word for more prophesy, let's look at some more of His promises. You must know of His promises to claim them. In Isaiah 43:26, God is talking, telling us.

"Put me in remembrance: Let us plead together: declare thou, that thou mayest be justified."

Our Father instructs His children to remind Him of His promises. No, God does not forget them. He wants to know if you know of them. In other words, have you taken the time to read His word to discover and be able to bring them up to Him, thus showing yourself justified (approved)? In Isaiah 1:18, God promises us that He will always listen. God states, *"Come now and let us reason together."* In other words, God is saying, I am reasonable, let's just talk about it. That is all prayer really is, just talking to Our Father. He does not want some scripted prayer written by someone else, and you sure don't need some man to be your go between or to tell you your sins are forgiven. That is a very dangerous practice. Our Father is very approachable. God Himself said in Jeremiah 17:5.

"Thus saith the Lord: Cursed be the man that trusteth in man," and in Jeremiah 17:7,

"Blessed is the man that trusteth in the Lord and whose hope is in the Lord."

The common denominator here is that you do not need to go through a man, any man, to pray and certainly not to repent for your sins. Hail Marys and Our Fathers will not do it. Repentance means a heart-felt change, and God knows what is in your heart.

Our Father may be disappointed with some of the things we do, but He is not mad at us. He loves us. He does not get up every day looking to zap one of His children. It broke His heart that we had to be in flesh. He wants to forgive us, as is documented in the second part of Isaiah 1:18.

"Though your sins be as scarlet, they shall be as white as snow; though they be red like crimson, they shall be as wool."

In other words, no matter how bad you messed up, just come clean and repent. In Matthew 18:21-22, Christ states that we can be forgiven as many as 490 times a day (seven multiplied by seventy). Seven is spiritual completeness. I do not recommend pushing this envelope, but it makes the point. Our Father wants to have a conversation. Just talk it over, documentation Isaiah 41:21.

"Produce your cause, saith the Lord; bring forth your strong reasons."

God knows what we need before we even ask. However, if you feel strongly about something, do not be afraid to make your request. But as you read for yourself, be prepared to justify your position. Does this sound like the unreasonable authoritarian some would lead us to believe God is? Unfortunately, this precept, or better stated, tradition of men, is still taught by some today. Our Father is well aware of this, as we see in Isaiah 29:13.

"Wherefore the Lord said, Forasmuch as this people draw near to me with their mouth, and with their lips do honor me, but have removed their heart far from me, and their fear toward me is taught by the precept (traditions) *of men."*

God does not want us to fear Him. He wants us to revere (to stand in awe of) Him. One of my two favorite promises in God's word is found in Isaiah 43:25.

"I even I, am He that blotted out thy transgressions (sins) *for My own sake, and I will not remember thy sins."*

This is truly great news. Our Father not only forgives our sins – He is telling us he chooses not to remember them and all for His sake. Our Father forgives and forgets. God is a parent, and those of us who are parents can certainly understand where He is coming from. This is just my opinion, but sometimes I think one of the reasons God put us in flesh bodies is so that we could know what it is like to be a parent. You know, just like our parents told us, "wait until you have kids then you will see." It is something to think about.

'Blotted out' means that our sins are gone – it is as if they never existed. In Hebrews 6:6, Paul tells us that to bring up sins already repented for is like re-crucifying Christ. Once was enough. We as humans will remember the experience, but only as a deterrent to repeating our mistakes. Do not bring them up to God ever again. The second of my favorite promises are in Hebrews 13:5 and Luke 10:19.

Hebrews 13:5 *"I will never leave you nor forsake you."*

This ties in with 1 Corinthians 10:13.

"There hath no temptation taken you but such that is common to man: but God is faithful, who will not suffer you to be tempted above that you are able; but will with the temptation also make a way to escape, that you may be able to bear it."

In other words, Our Father will never quit on us, and there is nothing going to happen to you that does not happen to everyone. God will never give us more then we can handle, and He will always show us a way out. As with most of God's promises, there is a condition. A small word with a huge meaning, if. IF we ask with faith, believing. Unshakable faith and belief grow from a deeper knowledge in God's word, as documented in Hebrews 11:6.

"But without faith it is impossible to please God: for he that cometh (with a request) *to God must believe that God is* (that He exists), *and that He is a rewarder of them that diligently seek Him."*

The message in this promise should be obvious to anyone who reads it. The simple fact is that if you do not believe in God, why would you pray to ask Him for anything in the first place? And the flip side is, why would God acknowledge a faithless request? Our Father knows what we are thinking. Consequently, He is acutely aware of one of His own creation's faith level. Never forget that we are instructed to seek the truth (knowledge) and truth in God's word. Through the Holy Spirit, you must work to increase your faith. We have to make the effort. Faith is the lynch pin to reaping God's blessings. It means everything. The above verse is a promise from God – it is something that we have already been given and need only faith to claim it. Luke 10:19 tells us in the verse below that Christ has given us power over satan and his demons. We simply do not have to put up with them bothering us.

"Behold I give you power (authority) *to tread on serpents and scorpions, and over all the power of the enemy: and nothing by any means shall hurt you."*

This applies only if you have faith. There are some skeptics who will say that the Old Testament does not apply to us today, and for this reason, and some other reasons, will not acknowledge it. This belief is simply not true and is a crying shame. Personally, I think that some refuse to study it. This is a shame. Most of the prophesies and promises you have just read are from the Old Testament. Christ quoted from the Old Testament many times and was Himself a fulfillment of prophesy from it, states Isaiah 7:14 in the Old Testament states,

"Therefore the Lord Himself shall give you a sign; behold, a virgin shall conceive, and bear a son, and shall call His name Immanuel."

This prophesy was written 630 years before the Christ's birth took place. No men could script this. According to Isaiah 48:5.

"I have even from the beginning declared it to thee, before it came to pass, I showed it to thee."

And as Matthew 1:23, in the New Testament reads,

"Behold a virgin shall be with child, and shall bring forth a son and they shall call His name Emmanuel."

Interpreted, Emmanuel means 'God with us'. Do not just read over this – something spectacular has happened. God, Our Father, has just taken on a flesh body. Imagine that. God is so fair and loving that He would not put us through something that He Himself is not willing to go through. And look at what the Kenites (satan's children) did to Him. We must never forget that the battle is between God and satan and that satan started it. While we are on the subject of Christ and the crucifixion, let's explore some more prophesy that takes us to that monumental event that brought about redemption and changed the way time is recorded, i.e., B.C. to A.D., in Psalms 22:1.

"My God, My God, why hast Thou forsaken Me?'

These words should be familiar to most. They are the exact words Christ spoke on the cross. However, the words above were written nearly 1000 years prior to the crucifixion. Scholars do not dispute this. If it is written, it will happen as it is written. The fulfillment of this prophesy is recorded in the New Testament Matthew 27:46.

"Eli, Eli, lame sabachthani?"

That is to say (which means in English), 'My God, My God, why hast thou forsaken Me?' It is taught by some, out of ignorance, that Christ was having a moment of weakness or doubt here. Not so. As you read the remaining verses in Psalms 22, it is apparent that Christ was quoting from this chapter while hanging on the cross. How beautiful, Christ Our Father in flesh was teaching, even as the life was so painfully being drained from His body.

There is prophesy that comes to mind and is actually in a parable. Christ spoke in parables many times. A parable is a short metaphorical story, in which there is a veiled truth. Not all are supposed to understand as is demonstrated in John 8:42-44 Christ talking to the Kenites. God simply does not want the enemy to understand certain secrets. I feel the need to remind you that the Kenites earned their burdens in the first earth age. God does put blinders on some of His children. He does this for their own protection. John 8:42.

"Jesus said unto them (the Kenites)*, 'If God were your Father, you would love Me."*

Verse 44. *"You are of your father, the devil, and the lusts of your father you will do."*

He was a murderer from the beginning. Cain was the first murderer and the first son of the devil (serpent). This bunch Christ is talking to here is in satan and Cain's lineage (Genesis 5). It does not get any clearer than this. Now, Christ is speaking to us in John 8:42.

"Why do you not understand my speech? Even because you cannot hear (understand) *My words."*

The Kenites are not able to grasp the deeper meaning in Christ's parables, and this is why He uses parables. It really is not as unfair as it sounds. There were numerous times when the disciples did not get it either, and the following parable is one of those times. Let us read it now.

The parable we are about to read, The parable of the tares, covers a very long period of time and is one that I doubt you will ever hear, in its entirety, from any pulpit. It starts in the Garden of Eden and concludes with the end of this world age. A portion of the prophesies in this parable have already been fulfilled, while others are yet future. Christ is speaking to a large gathering, and the disciples are with Him. The disciples were unable to grasp the meaning of this parable. See if you can grasp it, and if not, we will let Christ explain it for us in verses 36-43.

Matthew 13:24. *"Another parable He put forth unto them, saying that the kingdom of heaven is likened unto a man which sowed a good seed in His field,"*

It is important to understand that "the good seed" was planted by God Himself and goes all the way back to the Garden of Eden. The word "seed" used here in the original Greek is "sperma." We are not dealing with fairy tales.

Verse 25. *"But while men slept, His enemy came and sowed tares among the wheat, and went his way."*

The enemy spoken of here is the devil. It is going to be important that you understand exactly what tares are, metaphorically and in reality, or you will miss the point of this lesson. "Tares" or zewan, as they are known today in Palestine, while growing, look exactly like wheat. Even experts have difficulty telling them apart. However, when full grown, the tares' ears are long and the grains almost black. Each grain of zewan must be removed before grinding, because they are bitter and can be poisonous. Wheat is golden, but tares show their true color in the end as they ripen. This parable written some 2000 years ago is being fulfilled today. Continue reading and find out exactly what I mean. Verse 26.

"But when the wheat was sprung up, and brought forth fruit,

then appeared the tares, also."

Christ told us metaphorically, in Matthew 7:20.

"We are to judge a tree (man) by his fruit (works), *and not just what he says."*

They are certainly words to live by, in these end times. Matthew 13:27, below.

"So the servants of the Householder came and said to Him, Sir didst not thou sow good seed in Thy field? From whence then has it tares?"

They are asking where the tares came from. The tares represent the devils children from the sin in the Garden.

Matthew 13:28. *"He said unto them, An enemy hath done this. The servants said unto Him, wilt Thou then that we go and gather them up?* In other words; Should we rip them up?

Matthew 13:29. *"But He said, nay; lest while you gather up the tares, you root up also the wheat with them."*

Imagine a wheat field peppered with these poisonous tares. It would be impossible to pluck one up without uprooting and killing the surrounding wheat. We know that the good sower is God, and the enemy is the devil (serpent) but you must know the field is this world and this earth age. But if you don't, do not feel bad; again, the disciples did not get it either, however, they were not living in the end days as I believe we are. The tares represent the Kenites. This may be a digression, however it needs to be said. We know the Kenites are the offspring of satan. What you must understand is the Kenites throughout thousands of years have mixed with every race on this earth making, in some cases, identifying them extremely difficult. Here is a word to the wise. As tares show their true colors in the end so it may be with the Kenites of today. What do you mean? Are the Kenites of today starting to rear their poisonous black heads? I am in no way talking skin color, no way! I am talking about the black "head" masks that today's terrorists wear, after all they do not wear uniforms. These spawn of satan try to blend in with the wheat, (those who love Our Father). Could this explain why so many from free countries are swarming to terrorism? Just a thought. We have been told that all remaining prophesy will be fulfilled in these end times. It is not hopeless for the tares, John 3:16 is where their salvation lies. *"For God so loved the world, that He gave His only begotton son, that whosoever believeth in Him should not perish* (burned in the lake of fire), *but have everlasting life."* That is eternal life. Back to Matthew 13:30 to continue.

"Let both grow together until the harvest: and in the time of the harvest I will say to the reapers, gather ye together first the tares, and bind them in bundles to burn them: but gather the wheat into my barn.'"

This verse is describing what happens at the end of this world age and just before the millennium begins. How can we be sure? The angels only bind the tares to be burned. They will not be burned yet. With the exception of the fallen angels, no souls will be destroyed until the end of the millennium and after The Great White Throne Judgment. Verse 39 of Matthew 13 tells us that the reapers are God's angelic army, the same army Christ brings with Him when He returns at the end of this world (earth) age. Our Father knows the hearts of men who say they are good and are for that good, but they lie and are not. The tares are burned in the Lake of Fire at the end of the 1,000-year millennium (Revelation 20:15), never to be thought of again. The good children will, at that same time, be gathered into God's barn, heaven, for the Eternity.

As stated previously, this parable would be impossible to explain accurately, without the knowledge of what actually took place in the Garden at the beginning of this earth age. However, because we know from Genesis 3:16 that there was a conception at that time, there can be no doubt as to how the tares got on this earth. Never forget, the tares are not those who are not saved. They are the children of the devil. Those are Christ's words, not mine. This parable also answers the age old question asked by everyone at some time in their lives, especially during the chaos in these end days. That question is this: Will all mankind ever be able to get along, peacefully? The answer to this question is the classic good news/bad news scenario and is hidden within the parable we have just studied. No, there will never be true continuity among mankind in this earth age, as Genesis 3:15, the first prophesy in the Bible states,

"And I (God) *will put enmity* (hatred) *between thee* (satan) *and the woman* (Eve)*, and between thy seed (*offspring) *and her seed."*

Never forget this is with the exception of antichrist's 5 month reign. Enmity means hatred. As long as there are tares (satan's children, Kenites) in the world, there will be no true peace. There will be a brief time of false peace at the very end of this earth age. This is the time you want to be on your toes, because satan, as antichrist, ushers in a false peace and prosperity by claiming to be the true Jesus Christ. This false peace was spoken of by Daniel the prophet and reinforced by the Apostle Paul in 1 Thessalonians 5:3. First, let's look at Daniel 11:21.

"And in his estate shall stand up a vile person (antichrist*) to whom they shall not give the honor of the kingdom* (rule of this world)*: but* (except) *he shall come in peaceably and obtain the kingdom by flatteries."*

The antichrist will be a good-looking, sweet-talking, peaceful man (ish/ supernatural), and it makes sense. Once again, satan, as antichrist during the tribulation, will be claiming to be Christ returned. Daniel in verse 28 of this same chapter, tells us the antichrist will be able to do exploits, which when properly translated means 'miracles.' This is important, so let's explore it a little. A witness to the claim that the antichrist will be capable of performing miracles can be found in Revelation 13:13-14.

"And he (satan) *doeth wonders* (miracles), *so that he maketh fire come down from heaven onto the earth in the sight of men."*

Verse 14 nails it. *"And deceives them that dwell on the earth by means of those miracles, which he has the power to do."*

Satan, as antichrist, will be able to snap his fingers and, on his command, cause lightening to bolt down from heaven, and no doubt other miracles as well. Who is prepared for this? Not many. The largest denomination in the world totals more than a billion in numbers. Its leaders need only to witness three miracles as proof of God's intervention. All this is determined by a few men. That is a very dangerous situation considering God's warning concerning putting your trust in man.

Okay, using God's word and a little common sense in agriculture, you now know the true meaning of the parable of the tares. You are in rare company indeed. If you want, run it by a Man of the Cloth and listen for the answer. It is my guess that they will not know, certainly not to the depth you now know. If they should say they know, ask them why they don't teach it. Always be respectful. In either case, their sheep (following) will be as sheep to the slaughter when the antichrist arrives. God warned us this very thing would happen in Jeremiah 10:21.

"For the pastors are become brutish (stupid), *and have* not sought the Lord: (His word) *therefore they shall not prosper, and their flocks shall be scattered."*

Judgment begins at the pulpit. I only bring this up in the off chance that anyone tries to tell you that you do not need to know what is going to happen in the end days, because you are going to be out of here (The Rapture). They are wrong. We will debunk the rapture theory later in the last chapter, but for now let's examine some prophesy that is expressly relevant to the end times, the very times we are living in. The prophet Amos tells us that the famine in the end times will be for hearing the word of God. Amos 8:11.

"Behold the days come, saith the Lord God, that I will send a famine in the land, not a famine for bread, nor a thirst for water, but for hearing the words of the Lord."

This prophesy is being fulfilled today all around the world, especially with regard to the rising tide of the Muslim (extremist) religion. This is certainly not a safe time to be a Christian (Christ man) in the Middle East. Further, disdain for Christianity seems to be on the increase in Europe, Australia and the United States.

Although this country is more than 75 percent Christian, it is becoming increasingly apparent that there are some today who are just plain offended by anything having to do with God. There was a parallel to this scenario in the first earth age. Toward the end of that age, as with this one, the deviant minority dictated policy, while the majority sat idly on their hands. You know how that worked out for us. If you look around today it is not hard to see that there is a dedicated and coordinated effort being made to push God from every facet of our lives. Our children cannot pray in most public schools. The Ten Commandments are banned from our, not just their, public buildings. Nativity scenes are under constant attack, and a host of other intrusions are making the prophesies of Amos come to reality right before our very eyes. If you think there will not ever be an atheist push directed at churches, you need to think again. Just recently there was an attempt by a Houston Mayor to subpoena the sermons of pastors because she and others did not like their messages. She was attempting to disqualify their 503C tax exemption. You must be aware that attempts such as these are made to look as though they are the opinion of the majority by using the internet.

The purpose of this book is not political but politics and religion are biblically linked as is education and the economy. The Bible refers to these 4 entities as "the four hidden dynasties." Satan is allowed to infiltrate and use these 4 entities to further his plan. It should be obvious to anybody that he most certainly has. Religion certainly fits the topic when talking about the famine in the end times. Whether you agree or disagree with my previous stated examples there can be no question that satan is winning in the religious category and I offer my book as proof. I am willing to bet that the vast majority of the truths you have been reading you never knew. I do not say this to demine anyone because 99% of the world is unaware of them. That means 99% of the world is starving for this truth and that is the famine in these end days. This is famine and satan is to blame. At the risk of once again sounding political, I have to bring up a prophesy that is being fulfilled at this very time. This prophesy is found in Isaiah 3:4, Our Father speaking,

"And I will give children to be their princes (leaders), *and babes shall rule over them."*

Their = us, the loyal subjects of the world. 'Princes' is a metaphor for leaders, today's leaders. This prophesy reflects the whole world at this time, but nowhere is it as true as with the current leadership, and I use the word leadership loosely, in this once great country of ours. One has to wonder if there is an adult anywhere in the room. God 1000 years ago knew this would be the situation. Another all too applicable prophesy is found in Isaiah 5:20.

"Woe unto them that call evil good, and good evil; that put darkness for light, and light for darkness; that put bitter for sweet, and sweet for bitter."

The subject of this verse is warnings for the end times. Do you see anything like that going on today? What God is telling us here is that things in the end time will be upside down, wrong is right as per satan's plan. We work for our government officials and not the other way around as it was meant to be. Our government in this great country, the last bastion of true freedom, has become a beast as prophesied. It is in every facet of our lives, i.e. healthcare. And it is attempting to gain more control. God saw this coming.

Our Father is so very fair. He always gives us types of situations and individuals to sharpen our prophetic senses and to keep us alert on our watch for the antichrist. You always want to be suspicious of any man of power that speaks great platitudes and who talks as a peach tree, but produces only rotten figs. We are getting so very close to the end, and the first beast that exists now is governmental, socialism. The more people that are dependent on any government when this beast gets a deadly wound putting people on their financial knees, the easier it will be for satan as antichrist to persuade them to worship him when he heals this first beasts wound, causing them to worship him. Some other prophesy that comes to mind concerning these end days can once again be found in the Book of Isaiah, specifically in Isaiah 29:15.

"*Woe to them that seek deep to hide their counsel from the Lord* (and the people)*, and their works are in the dark, and they say, who seeth us*? *And who knoweth us*?"

God knows what our and the world's leaders are doing behind closed doors. They will be judged for their actions. Come, Lord, Come. We are in the birth (labor) pains of this earth age. As is unique to labor pains, they come on closer and closer together with greater intensity as the birth nears. In our case it is the birth of a new age, the millennium. Once the birth pains start, they do not stop as documented in Isaiah 66:9.

"Shall I bring to the birth, and not cause to bring forth? Saith the Lord: *"Shall I cause to bring forth, and shut the womb?"* Saith the Lord God.

There will always be those who say it is not happening and it is not going to happen. God knows who they are. We see in Jeremiah 14:13.

"Then said I (Jeremiah), Lord God! Behold the (false) *prophets that say unto them, you shall not see the sword, neither shall you have famine."*

Do not believe them believe your Father. What does Our Father have to say to these skeptics? He tells us in Ezekiel 12:25.

"I am the Lord: I will speak and the word that I shall speak shall come to pass; it shall no more be prolonged: for in your days, O rebellious house (us), I will say the word, and will perform it, saith the Lord God!"

God's word is true. He has told us everything we need to know pertaining to the end of this world age. Those of us who love Our Father have nothing to worry about. We WIN.

CHAPTER 6

TWO BODIES, TWO DEATHS

Christ tells us in Mark 12:27, *"God is not the God of the dead, but the God of the living."*

No human beings ever born in flesh are truly dead. Dead is a concept man has thought up because of his ignorance in God's word. In order to fully understand the biblical meaning of "the dead" and their whereabouts, you must be capable of going to the spiritual level of Our Father's word.

In order to grasp the concept and discover where the dead really are, it is essential that you understand that everyone ever created by God has two bodies. Two bodies but only one soul. Your soul is real. It is that which makes you, you. Your intellect or spirit. In the first book of Corinthians Chapter 15, Paul gives the best example of this fact subject being, our two bodies. I have in a previous chapter documented Paul's undeniable credibility. Paul is God's chosen vessel. Let us begin our search for the truth regarding this matter in 1 Corinthians 15:35 and pick up the subject of the following verses, our two bodies.

Verse 35 is a good example of how a subject can change in the middle of a chapter:

"But some man will say, How are the dead raised up? And with what body do they come?"

Paul in the verse following, makes us aware of the inevitability of this question by his tone in the next verse. This question will come up when you are planting seeds and you need to know the answer. So let's look at verse 36.

"Thou fool, that which thou sowest is not quickened (made alive) *except it die."*

Paul is a tough, street smart, straight talking man, not one given to mincing his words. Paul himself, in 2 Corinthians 11:6, reveals that he is rude in speech. Paul's day job is that of a tent maker, and he is the proverbial salt of the earth. Paul spoke colloquial Greek, street Greek if you will. It is for this reason that he is difficult to understand. The answer to this question, based on Paul's short quip 'thou fool,' is something that has been discussed before and is very important. That Paul thinks understanding the question is important is good enough for me. Sowest means that one body (the flesh body) must die. Quickened means 'to make alive'. The following verse lets us know what God thinks about cloning. Verse 38 reads,

"But God giveth it (soul) *a body as it has pleased Him, and to every seed His* (their) *own body."*

It is a soul. The soul is a flesh body's internal intellect. It is that which makes you, you. Notice God gives the soul. He reserves this privilege for Himself alone. Ezekiel Ch. 18:4 states that all souls belong to God.

Verse 39. *"All flesh is not the same flesh: But there is one kind of flesh of men, and another flesh of beasts, another of fishes, and another of birds."*

Paul digresses here to make His point, but all these creatures have one thing in common. They all belong to God. This begs the question: Do animals have souls? I do not know for sure but God's word tells us that there will be animals in the Eternity in Isaiah 11:6 and Isaiah 65:25, just to name two. We now know that there were animals in the first earth age, we find their fossilized remains everywhere. In 1 Corinthians 15:50-52, Paul tells us that flesh and blood cannot enter heaven. This information tells us that animals as well as humans will shuffle off their mortal coils (flesh bodies) and put on immortality. And last but not least, Genesis 1:20 begins the fifth day of creation, when God says.

"Let the waters bring forth abundantly the moving creature that has life, and foul (birds)."

The word 'life' used here in the manuscripts is nephesh, which translated means 'soul'.

Verse 21 tells us, *"And God created whales, and every living creature that moveth."*

Once again the word 'creature', as it is used here, in the original manuscripts is nephesh or soul. You decide for yourself. The answer to this question will not make or break your chance at the Eternity. I only bring it up to stir up the gray matter between your ears. We do know for a fact that there will be animals in heaven. Our Father loves His animals, back to 1 Corinthians 15:40.

"There are also celestial bodies, and bodies terrestrial: but the glory of the celestial is one, and the glory of the terrestrial is another."

Here you have it, as clear as Paul could make it. We have two bodies, and they are separate and different. Terrestrial means 'of the earth,' as in terra firma, your flesh body. Celestial is of the heavens and is your eternal body with Christ in Paradise. However, Paradise has two sides to it with a gulf separating the two sides that no one can cross. The right side of paradise is for those who overcome in this flesh age. The left side of Paradise is for those who do not overcome in this age. Is this why Christ told us to fish out of the right side of the boat? You can read about Paradise and the gulf in between in The Book of Luke Chapter 16 starting with verse 19, the story of the rich man and Lazarus, the poor beggar. It will be important as you read that you keep in mind Christ's words to the repetitive malefactor on the cross. *"This day you will be with Me in Paradise."* Paradise not heaven.

There is some subtle evidence in the rich man and the beggar lesson, although on opposite sides of Paradise, the beggar and Abraham, as well as the rich man, are very much alive in their (other) eternal bodies. All three have passed on from their flesh bodies. The rich man because of his actions in a flesh body has landed on the wrong side of Paradise. He is allowed to look across the gulf and see what he has missed. He will be there until the end of the millennium. This man is not in hell, he instead is burning with remorse and the water he so desperately desires is spiritual water, the truth in God's word. Do not end up like the rich man, learn that truth today. This is a great example why you should not speed read the Bible (Our Father's letter to His children). Conclusion: Two separate bodies, two separate deaths.

I am going to mention this now in case I forget to later. When Christ returns to this earth at the seventh trumpet's warning, He brings only the people on the Right side of Paradise along with Him. These are those who have been tested, in the flesh and in whom He knows He can trust with total freedom. Those on the left side of Paradise will remain on that side, unable to leave, until the thousand years of the millennium are accomplished. During the millennium, those on the left will be taught by those on the right. What will be taught? God's word, the very word you are reading right now, and discipline. Our Fathers word is the same today as it was in the beginning and will be throughout the Eternity. Exposing the antichrist and his plan will most certainly guarantee your seat on the right side of Paradise. I will share one more verse from Paul to nail it, with 1 Corinthians 15:53.

"For this corruptible must put on incorruption, and this mortal must put on immortality."

Paul in verse 53 and 54 is not being redundant or repetitive. In verse 53, Paul is referring to bodies. In verse 54, he is referring to the soul that is within everybody. Remember, there are two deaths. When someone dies in the flesh, there is a judgment made. People die every day thus there is judgment every day. This judgment, or assessment, is not to be confused with The Great White Throne Judgment at the end of the millennium. This judgment is only to determine which side of the gulf between Paradise someone goes. Once in Paradise, they remain in their other (celestial or angelic) bodies with their incorruptible (eternal) or mortal soul. Mortal means, liable to die, and incorruptible means that you made it. You overcame and you are in the express lane to the Eternity. Those who overcame will be teachers throughout the millennium documentation (Ezekiel 44:23 and Revelation 20:6). Hint, priest, prophet or pastor in the original Hebrew simply means "teacher." During the millennium those that did not overcome in the flesh will be taught by those that overcame. Those on the wrong side of paradise have to remain there until the end of the millennium. It is not until the end of the millennium, after satan has once again been loosed for a short period of time, to test only those on the left side of Paradise, those with corruptible or mortal souls, that The Great White Throne Judgment takes place. It is at that time that those who failed the second test, along with satan and his system, are thrown into the Lake of Fire never to be heard from again. To those who have made it, this is when our rewards are handed out. I said rewards, not punishment. This is the beginning of the Eternity.

Now that we can be sure we have two bodies, let's turn to the book of Revelation and learn more about the second death and the millennium.

Saint John wrote Revelation in the year 96 A.D. Saint John was taken from the Isle of Patmos where he was being held in irons. John was shown the events that will take place at the end of this world age (to the future...right about now judging by current events). The actual name of this book is "The Revelation of Jesus

Christ," so we know it can be trusted, Revelation 20:1.

"And I saw an angel come down from heaven, having the key of the bottomless pit and a great chain in his hand."

The angel here is Michael, the archangel. The time frame: the seventh trumpet has just sounded, and Christ has just returned with His army and defeated satan. The flesh age is finished. This is the first instant of the millennium, and at this time, all remaining souls are changed into their other, eternal, celestial bodies. 1 Corinthians 15:52 tells us this happens "in an instant, in the twinkling of an eye." All souls are in their celestial bodies, however, they are still on this very earth. Those on the left side of Paradise will now be brought to this earth, after Christ's return. The earth will exist as we know it now. This earth is not rejuvenated until after the millennium ends (Revelation 21:1).

It is for this reason I do not believe there will be a nuclear holocaust. If we are to inhabit this earth during the millennium, it will have to be inhabitable, as in not all blown to hell. Considering what is going on in the world today, I believe the end is very near and here is one reason. This is my opinion. You have a country in the Middle East today that swears when it gets Nuclear Weapons they will blow Jerusalem off the face of this earth. This country will be allowed to develop nukes but will be stopped just short of launching them at Jerusalem. Why? Mt. Zion in Jerusalem is where Christ will sit on His throne during the millennium. I do not believe, if nuked, this location would be inhabitable in flesh or celestial bodies. Revelation 20:2 says.

"And He laid hold of the dragon, that old serpent, which is the devil, and satan, and bound him a thousand years."

Christ has just defeated satan and his one-world religious system at the sounding of the 7th trumpet. The fallen angels are at this time destroyed. Now Michael will lock up satan for the duration of the millennium. Satan, in the millennium will have 0 influence in person or in spirit. Notice the various names for the devil. We can be positive this is the same serpent that impregnated Eve in the Garden, as we examine Verse 3 of revelation Ch. 20.

"And cast him (the antichrist) into the bottomless pit, and shut him up, and set a seal upon him, that he should deceive nations no more, until the thousand years are fulfilled: and after that he must be loosed a little season."

There is so much information being given in this verse it has to be broken down. Michael locks satan securely in the bottomless pit. He then, with God's approval, places a seal upon satan. This seal is very important. It not only locks up satan's body, but also his spirit. At this present time in this flesh age, satan's spirit is allowed to traverse the earth. This is fair, because God's Spirit, the Holy Spirit, is also present and available to us on this earth at this time.

This flesh age is a test, and every positive needs a negative. Think about this. In the millennium there will be absolutely no (that is zero) negative influence from satan. Couple that with the fact that no one will be in a flesh body. This will give those on the wrong side of paradise a huge advantage. There will be no flesh constantly nagging at them. Sins of the flesh will simply not exist. It is for this reason that more souls will be saved during the millennium than at any other time in creation. This just reinforces how much Our Father loves His children. He gives them every chance to make the Eternity while weeding out any who might ever cause grief or anything like this flesh test again.

God, Our Father, loves us. He may not love what we do sometimes, but He does love us. Remember, He does not get up every day looking to zap someone. He simply wants us to do our best and love Him. Never forget that it broke His heart to do this in the first place, but it had to be done. We do not have to be perfect. God considers an honest try perfect. Just try, and know that forgiveness is only a heartfelt thought away, which verse 4 of Revelation 20 assures.

"And I (Saint John) *saw thrones, and they that sat upon them; and I saw the souls of them that were beheaded for the witness of Jesus, and for the word of God, and which had not worshiped the beast, neither his image, neither had received his mark upon their foreheads, or in their hands; and they lived and reigned with Christ a thousand years."*

John is in the millennium and is being shown those who sit on thrones and will assist God in the first judgment, as well as the martyrs from this flesh age. The judgment at the end of the millennium, the second, The Great White Throne Judgment, will be by God alone. Take particular note at the mention of those who did not worship the beast. The beast mentioned here is the religious system that satan ushers in upon his arrival on this earth. Those who overcame the antichrist and his system were those not deceived into taking his mark. 'On' is a bad translation. It should be translated as 'in'. This mark (the mark of the beast) is not on ones forehead, *it is in ones forehead.*

What is in your forehead? Your brain. If you have the truth, this truth that we are studying right now, sealed in your forehead, you will not be fooled into worshiping the antichrist. It is as simple as that. Let us face it – someone could tattoo you from head to toe with 666, and it would not change your belief. Would it? The mark will not be a microchip in your hand, either. The reference to hand here represents working. Working in this case, by helping satan's religious movement along. Again, he will be claiming to be Christ and playing church. Tell me, who doesn't like to help out the church? Those who overcome this very ingenious deception will reign with Christ for the duration of the millennium, one thousand years, according to verse 5.

"But the rest of the dead lived not again until the thousand years were finished."

We have already covered this. However, verses like this are why so many say that the *Bible* is so difficult to understand. I agree, so let's make sense of it. The dead being talked about in this verse are those who were deceived by antichrist or who died before his arrival and lived a life that did not allow them to overcome. These souls are spiritually dead, as in their souls are mortal or liable to die, as has been discussed. It will not be until the millennium is finished, that the decision will be final. If they overcome satan's second tribulation at the end of the millennium, their souls become immortal. They are alive and will live with God as well as the rest who overcame, forever and ever. Those who fail the second test will after the Great White Throne Judgment, spiritual body and soul, be destroyed in the Lake of Fire, as is clearly stated in Revelation 20:14.

"And death and hell were cast into the Lake of Fire."

This is the second death. And whosoever was not found written in the book of life was cast into the Lake of Fire. They, as well as any memory of them, will be blotted out, Psalms 69:28 reads.

"*Let them be blotted out of the book of the living* (eternally)."

"Blotted out" means it will be as though they never existed. We will have absolutely no recollection of them or their existence. How will God do this? No doubt, the same way He blocked our recollection of the first earth age. Revelation 20:6.

"Blessed and holy is he that has part in the first resurrection: on such the second death hath no power, but they shall be priests of God and Christ, and shall reign with Him a thousand years."

By now you should be able to interpret most of this verse for yourself. The first resurrection comes immediately after the death of ones flesh body in 1 Corinthians 5:6-7. Paraphrasing, 'absent from your flesh body' is to be present with the Lord in your eternal body. There is no in between. They are alive (spiritually) and well. Those on the right side teaching those on the left side of paradise. Asleep is just an expression to describe the condition of being dead, as documented in Matthew 22:32.

"God is not the God of the dead, but the God of the living, whether in a flesh body or in an eternal body. Rejoice for those who have passed on, for them the test is over and they are back home with Christ."

This will be review but it is just that important. The death of your flesh body is a death that all who are born in a flesh body will experience. There is simply no escaping it. Whether you overcome or not, in the flesh (this flesh age) you go instantly into your eternal body at the beginning of the millennium, and that is understood. If at that time you are judged worthy, you go to the right side of Paradise. Those on the right side, because of their behavior in a flesh body, will never have to be judged again. They made it. Their place in the Eternity is secured. The second death at the end of the millennium has no effect on them. What you do in the millennium does however matter. Those that teach for example, will be helping God save souls and no good work goes without reward. Our Father owns everything and He intends to share it with His children. The "Great White Throne Judgment" the second judgment, is when we get our rewards.

The last part of Revelations 20:6 is where some explanation may be needed. Those who made the first resurrection still have work to do. Those who overcame are to be teachers (priests) to those who did not overcome in the flesh. Priest in the Hebrew language simply means 'teacher,' whether in this age or the millennium. A teacher is supposed to teach. Unfortunately, at our present moment in time they do not. I am guessing, but this may be the first time you are hearing most of what is being taught in this book. It is unfortunate, but it is better now than later. Getting back to Revelation 20:7.

"And when the thousand years (the millennium) *are expired,*

satan shall be loosed out of his prison."

This is additional documentation supporting what we have covered previously. At the very end of the millennium, and immediately before The Great White Throne Judgment, is another test only for those on the left side of Paradise. Remember, those on the right side of Paradise have made it. This test only concerns them inasmuch as they may have taught some who will be tested. I am sure they will be pulling for them.

Michael, at this time, will unlock the pit and remove the seal that was placed on satan at the millennium's beginning. It is not stated as to how long this tribulation will last, but God is fair, so it stands to reason it will not last longer then will the tribulation at the end of this flesh age. Once again, those who fail this time are out of here along with satan – and good riddance. We want only peace in the Eternity.

In conclusion, we all have two bodies, and they are different as well as separate. The death of our flesh bodies is inevitable. The death of our eternal or spiritual or celestial or immortal bodies is avoidable first by our actions in this second earth age, and if necessary by our actions in the millennium. The second death, the death of your soul in the Lake of Fire, is the death you want to avoid at all costs.

We thank Our Father for redemption where upon repentance (a heartfelt apology) we are forgiven, and our slate is wiped clean, never to be brought up again. In the next chapter I will explain step by step how it comes down in these end days confirming that satan is the antichrist.

CHAPTER 7

THE BEGINNING OF THE END

2 Corinthians 11:14. *"And no marvel; for satan himself is transformed into an angel of light."*

Paul is talking about satan's return as the antichrist at the end of this age. Satan is the great imitator – whatever names or actions are unique to Christ, the devil will emulate. Christ is our Light, light being symbolic of truth, the very truth that lights the way to eternal life, as stated in John 8:12.

"Then spake Jesus again unto them, saying, I am the light of the world: he that followeth Me shall not walk in darkness, but shall have the light of life." (Eternal).

It is for this reason satan calls himself the angel of light. Remember, he is a liar and the father of lies. In previous chapters, scripture from Our Father's word has been provided documenting that the end of this world age is *"neigh, at hand, right at the door."* As we head into this chapter, which by its title should give you some idea of where we are headed, I want to cite some scripture that is pertinent to the times we are living in and support it with current events.

We are, for a moment, going to be concentrating on the geographical location of the nation of Israel, specifically, the city of Jerusalem itself. The Bible contains much prophesy pertaining to Jerusalem in these end times and not by coincidence. Jerusalem is to be our barometer in these end days. It is where our Lord will sit on His throne for the millennium, immediately after the defeat of antichrist and his army. When reading the Bible you must know the difference between "Israel" the tribes of Israel and "Israel" the physical location.

We are told to keep a close eye on the events that are taking place in Jerusalem today, as well as those yet to unfold in this ancient city. In order for end time prophesy to come to its fulfillment, Israel would at the very least have to be a nation once again. Wouldn't you agree? That event took place in May of 1948. This monumental yet contentious event began "The Generation of The Fig Tree," spoken of by Jesus Christ 2,000 years before its fruition, Matthew 24:32. Let's go ahead and use the nation of Israel in tandem with the city of Jerusalem, contained within its borders, and place them in with recorded history to further substantiate my belief that we are most certainly in the end days.

The city of Jerusalem has been sacked or under siege 27 times. The 20th and probably best-known attack took place in 69 A.D. and was levied by the Roman General Titus. This invasion was so complete that the city lay desolate for 50 years and was all but forgotten. Some Bible historians believe this was fulfillment of Christ's prophesy from Matthew 24:2 and Mark 13:2. No way! Before we read through the aforementioned verses, allow me to set up the situation for you. Christ and His disciples have just left the temple in Jerusalem. Remember, they are country boys and therefore thoroughly amazed by the magnificent buildings, as is evident when one of the twelve comments on his observation in Mark 13:1.

"And as they went out of the temple, one of His disciples saith unto Him, 'Master, see what manner of stones and what buildings are here'!"

And in verse 2: *"And Jesus answering said unto him, 'Seest thou these great buildings? There shall not be left one stone upon another, that shall not be thrown down'."*

Christ states that not one stone will be standing. After the 69 A.D. attack there were still many stones left standing. Most predominantly, the Wailing Wall still stands, at least as of this writing. This is a digression but I feel that the Wailing Wall will be where the two witnesses will be killed. That is just my opinion and therefore we are to be watchmen. Titus's attack, although devastating, would not be the last against Jerusalem by any means. Fifty years after Titus' attack the city was rebuilt. There have been seven additional attacks against Jerusalem since, placing the total to date at 27. The fact that there will be a 28th is recorded in prophesy. The Book of Zachariah, Chapter 14 states that Christ Himself will wage this final battle, fulfilling the final capture of this holy city, Jerusalem. We are so very close. Prophesy also warns us in Luke 21:20 that when you see Jerusalem surrounded by her enemies, the end is near.

"And when you shall see Jerusalem compassed (surrounded) *with armies then know that the desolation* (destruction) *there of is nigh."*

There will be only one more attack on Jerusalem. The city is at this time surrounded by her enemies, and some who are on record as threatening to wipe her off the map. Have you ever wondered why the little city of Jerusalem seems to be the focus of everyone's attention in the world today? Jerusalem is God's favorite place in the universe. He married it figuratively speaking, in Ezekiel 16:8. Check it out. The act of spreading ones skirt over a woman symbolizes marriage and is still a custom in eastern countries today. Satan is well aware that Jerusalem is God's true love. Remember satan is the great imitator and Jerusalem is where Christ's throne will be throughout the millennium as well as where The God Head (the Father, the Son and the Holy Spirit as one) will set up His throne for the Eternity. Satan knows scripture very well and therefore knows he must eventually take control of Jerusalem. This will ultimately lead the world to Armageddon. The United States is the New Jer-USA-lem, a super power of super powers charged to protect Jerusalem. This is the first time in U.S. history a president has turned his back on this command from God. Another name for antichrist is "the lawless one." He is the model for narcissism. Any time you hear this know that the end is near. The fact that the antichrist will, for a short time, indeed sit in Jerusalem claiming to be Christ is well documented in 2 Thessalonians Ch. 2 verses 1-12.

By now you may have surmised that I believe we are in the very end of this, the second earth age. I believe this with my whole heart and soul, which is the primary reason I wrote this book. Let's face it – most people can feel something big brewing on the horizon. Let's let God's word reveal and explain some additional events that will take place to consummate the end of this earth age. I want to be clear, the end of this flesh earth age is in no way the end of this earth (world) as is documented in Ephesians 3:21, world without end, amen. The Eternity will be on this earth.

We will simply and instantly go from this age into the millennium, which will take place on this very earth, as it is. Ephesians was written by the Apostle Paul around 62 A.D. Paul wrote this epistle from Rome while he was in prison there. Unique to this writing is that this instance is the first time Paul elaborated on the heavenly mysteries (events) he was shown while on the road to Damascus. Prior to this, Paul had never spoken on record about the things he was shown that fateful day.

We will not only identify the events that consummate the end, but we will examine exactly how they will unfold. Be aware that after the occurrence of a certain event, we will be able to affix a time frame to those events that remain (see your chart "The sequence of events in the end times.") You are aware that God has foretold us all the things we need to know regarding the end of this earth age, as documented in Mark 13:23. Christ's own words,

"But take you heed: behold I have foretold you all things."

Keep in mind that the subject of the 13th chapter in the book of Mark is – When will this earth age end, and what will be the signs?

Never forget our Father has told us everything regarding this matter and He expects His children to learn it. In Isaiah 45:7, God is speaking:

"I form the light, and I create the darkness: I make peace, and create evil (calamity)*: I the Lord do all these things."*

What Our Father is telling us in this verse is that He is in control. If there is anything adverse going on, He knows. This age will end exactly when and how God planned it. Our Father is no more going to let us, His children, trash His earth than our parents would their house while they were on vacation. One phone call from the neighbors, and that was it. Back they came, and look out.

Those who love God have nothing to fear. He has a handle on everything, and nothing, by any means, gets by Him. The fight in this earth age is between Him and satan, and God Our Father will win! If for no other reason, this is why you want to be on the side of Our Father. God allows, and with some cases even directs satan's actions in this earth age. Why would He do that? Our Father does not want what happened in the first earth age to ever happen again. He needs to know beyond the shadow of a doubt which of His children truly love Him and can be trusted and which of those children can be deceived by satan. Does God cause wars? Yes, sometimes, as this verse documents, if it is necessary to further His plan. You can read of these conflicts for yourself in His Word.

We learned in the last chapter that there are two deaths. Consequently, we know that anyone who has ever died in this earth age, either by natural causes, or some other tragedy, are still very much alive spiritually, some more than others. However, it depends on what side of Paradise they landed. The point is, no soul God has ever created is as of yet doomed with the exception of satan and his fallen angels. They have already been judged and are sentenced to death. God tells us through the Apostle Peter in 1 Peter 4:7.

"We are to be as watchman, watching for those signs of the end of this age."

You cannot watch for signs if you do not know what those signs are. Genesis 1:14.

"And God said, let there be lights in the skies of the heavens, to divide the day from the night; and let them be for signs and for seasons, and for days, and for years." And so it is.

Some signs are and will be more obvious than others. For example, the four blood moons mean something, and it is ill-advised to overlook them. Blood moons are not all that rare in and of themselves, however, when there have been four of these moons in succession, all landing on High Holy Days, something important has always happened regarding Israel. The reestablishment of the nation of Israel in 1948 and the 1967 six-day war are two that come to mind.

However, there was another occurrence, not nearly as well known. Anyone who has ever completed the fourth grade knows what happened in 1492, but what is not widely known is that in that same year Spain expelled all Jews from the country just before the Spanish inquisition. This may or may not mean anything, but I believe that the United States of America is a type of Promised Land. I believe the USA is as the New Jerusalem. I have previously stated that the birth pains (sorrows) that bring about the end of this age have started. Hosea 13:13 confirms this. The subject of this verse concerns the end days.

"The sorrows of a traveling woman shall come upon them."

"Traveling" means a woman in the process of giving birth, or in labor. Mark Chapter 13, the chapter we are going to use as our outline tells us the wise in God's word that we are in the sorrows of the end days. What is unique to birth pains (pangs)? They come on closer and closer together and with increasing intensity, up until the birth. Something you must never forget, as it is a promise from God, is found in Isaiah 66:9, God speaking.

"Shall I bring to birth, and not cause to be born? Saith the Lord: shall I cause to bring forth and shut the womb? Saith thy God."

What Our Father is telling us here is that once the sorrows begin, they will not stop until the birth. In our case it is to be the birth of a new age, The MILLENNIUM. I believe it, as will you, when you are done reading this chapter. Your life in the Eternity depends on it.

Christ said He would become a stumbling block to those who love Him but lack knowledge in The Word of God. In other words, if you know of and love Jesus Christ, but you have never been taught that the false christ comes first instead of the True Christ, you will (not may) fall for the false christ. Romans 10:2 reads,

"For I bear them record that they have a zeal (enthusiastic love) *for God, but not according to knowledge."*

They (God's children) love Him, but they are ignorant. They have not been taught because very, very few people know of the truth. Priest in the Hebrew language simply means teacher. Pastors are to feed their sheep knowledge. Reverends claim a title reserved for Our Father alone. Ministers are to minister to the spiritual needs of their congregations. You get the idea. In defense of evangelists, their job is to bring people to Christ. It is the job of a teacher to take it from there.

If you do not know the truth, you will be deceived. The antichrist will be that good. He is not a mortal man. He is going to put on a show as never seen before. At this point in time people have just about seen it all. To anyone who thinks the antichrist will be a man – been there, done that. God's twist at the end of this age is perfect. There is no Mortal man that could get the whole world to follow him at this point in time, especially in a one-world religious movement. However, a supernatural being capable of performing truly awe worthy miracles, claiming to be Christ returned, is just what it will take. Think it through. After 9/11 our government, in an attempt to assess blame, came up with only one conclusion – the only thing lacking on our part was imagination. It is for this reason that I am SOUNDING THE ALARM. Father, let those who have an ear to hear, listen to the sound of the trumpets warning, as depicted in Joel 2:1.

"Blow you the trumpet in Zion (Mt. Zion, located in Jerusalem), *and sound an alarm in my Holy Mountain: let all the inhabitants of the land tremble: for the day of the Lord cometh, for it is nigh at hand."*

Here again, we have an excellent example as to why it is so important to pick up the subject and fix a time frame. "The Day of the Lord" is The Lord's Day. The Lord's Day is the Millennium. Here is how we can know. 2 Peter 3:8 tells us,

"That one day to the Lord is a thousand years to (mortal) *man."*

The millennium is 1,000 years. It is 1,000 years of teaching to those who did not overcome in this flesh age, as documented in Revelation 20:6. The millennium begins the very second that Christ's feet touch down on mount Zion at the sounding of the 7th trumpet, thus ending this earth age. Again, there is no gap – it is instantaneous. Any time it is written 'The Lord's Day,' you can be sure that it is talking about the millennium or judgment day.

Let's turn to the book of Mark and begin with Chapter 13. The Apostle Mark, a very young lad, was the cousin of Barnabas, also an Apostle. Mark's gospel is fast moving and vivacious, as you would expect from a young man tagging along with the Messiah as He taught and worked miracles. Mark, in thanks for his efforts to spread Christianity, was drug by horses until he was dead. Let us read for ourselves this martyr's account concerning the events in the last days in Mark 13:1.

Christ Himself is going to tell us:
WHEN WILL THIS WORLD AGE END?

Mark 13:1. *"And as he went out of the temple one of his disciples saith unto him, Master, see what manner of stones and what buildings are here!"*

Christ has just finished speaking in the temple, and his disciples are no doubt in awe at being inside of the walls of the great city of Jerusalem. Remember, they were country boys, and no doubt amazed at the buildings that existed within this city walls, as we see in Mark 13:2.

"And Jesus answering said unto him, Seeth thou these great buildings? There shall not be left one stone upon another, that shall not be thrown down."

Jerusalem has had a long history of destruction throughout her existence in this age. She has been singed and/or destroyed 27 times. We have documented there will be a 28th and final, according to Zechariah Chapter 14:2.

"Behold the day of the Lord cometh, and thy spoil shall be divided in the midst of thee."

Note the day of the Lord.

We know verse 2 is talking about the millennium or to God Judgment Day.

"For I will gather all nations against Jerusalem to battle; and the city shall be taken, and the houses rifled, and the women ravished; and half of the city shall go forth into captivity, and the residue of the people shall not be cut off from the city."

This above verse is describing Armageddon, the final battle of this earth age, and where it takes place, the valley of Mageddo just outside of Jerusalem. This is why we are told to watch what happens in and around Jerusalem. Again, Jerusalem is our barometer in these end times, as indicated in Zechariah verse 3.

"Then shall the Lord go forth, and fight against those nations, as when He fought in the day of the battle."

Here we have the case of a verse that without knowledge of the first earth age would be impossible to interpret correctly. *"the day of the battle "* is the katabole', the battle that ended the first earth age. Back to Mark 13:3.

"And as He (Christ) sat upon the Mt. Of Olives overlooking Jerusalem, Peter and James and John and Andrew asked him privately."

Apparently these four disciples were intrigued by Christ's comment. Christ and his disciples are sitting on the Mount of Olives, looking out over the Kedron Valley and into the city of Jerusalem a half mile to the west. This is where they spent a lot of time with Christ teaching them the truth of the ages, what has happened in days past as well as what is going to happen in the future. What an awesome experience, talking to and asking questions of God Our Father in the flesh, as we see happening in Mark 13:4.

"Tell us when shall these things be? And what shall be the sign when all these things shall be fulfilled?"

This is probably the most frequently asked question of all time. When will the end of this earth age (the flesh age) be, and how will we know? Christ, in the following verses of Mark 13, will answer these questions. Christ himself will give us the seven seals (the information describing the action or event that is about to happen), seven trumps (trumpets - a call to action or warning, as in 'to trumpet a charge' or to retreat), and the seven viles (the execution of the action itself). I believe we are currently in the fifth seal. The fifth seal is the learning seal. The sixth and next seal is when satan, as the antichrist, will be cast out of heaven along with the fallen angels and will be on this earth, as stated in Revelation 12:8-9:

"And (satan) *prevailed not, neither was there found place anymore in heaven. And the great dragon was cast out, that old serpent, called the devil, and satan, who will deceive the whole world: he was cast on to the earth and his angels were cast out with him."*

Do not read over the words "was cast." This is documentation that satan will not be born of woman. He will be in his spiritual body and a young man. Also "deceive the whole world." Satan as antichrist will be that convincing, however, there will be the exception. The exception is the Elect. God's Elect are those who know the truth and will not be deceived by antichrist when he returns. What is the truth? I am about to lay it out as clearly as I possibly can.

First, let's deal with the Elect. The Elect are those individuals who know the sequence of the events (those on your chart) that take place at the end of this earth age. The Elect are not necessarily the smartest or the best looking. They are those of God's children who stood with Him against satan during the rebellion in the first age and therefore He knows He can count on them again. The Elect are entrusted to hold the line and to bear witness of God's truth in this earth age. Because they were selected from the first age, God refers to them as His chosen in Isaiah 43:10. The testimony of the Elect will turn many of those deceived back to the real Christ. Isaiah 43:10.

"You are my witnesses, saith the Lord, and my servants Whom I have chosen," and Ephesians 1:4.

"According as He (God) *hath chosen us in Him before the foundations of the* (this) *world* (age)."

There has always been a remnant of Elect throughout this earth age. Those Elect that have come and have passed away did their job which was to keep the truth (this truth we are exposing) alive, from generation to generation until now. God has seen to it.

The Elect know that there was an age before this one, which allows them the background to process the full truth. The Elect also know that satan returns to this earth claiming to be Christ as documented in 2 Corinthians 11:14.

"And no marvel (wonder) *for satan himself is transformed* (disguised) *into an angel of light."* After all he is the great imitator.

The Elect know that satan will never be in a flesh body but will look to us to be a man (ish). He will be very good-looking (beautiful), not what so many have been led to expect, i.e., demonic being with horns and a tail. Antichrist will be charismatic and full of wisdom, and Ezekiel 28 tells us.

"He will be wiser then Daniel the prophet."

And why not? Satan still has total knowledge of the first earth age, while Daniel had only the knowledge that God supplied him in this age. It is quite possible satan may know you from that age. The antichrist will be able to perform miracles right in the sight of everyone watching. (Revelation 13:14). Imagine this scenario: satan as antichrist holds a one-world church revival, preaching and revealing secrets that most think only Christ could know.

This wolf in sheep's clothing will use flattery, not hostile threats, to woo the unenlightened world into his flock. With the same old stale and empty messages that today's men of the cloth are preaching, the antichrist's fertile pasture for the mind will look lush and green. Any uninformed sheep will follow the antichrist to their spiritual slaughter, because he is claiming to be Jesus Christ.

Do not be fooled, because the Antichrist is claiming to be Christ he will not get away with using violence to swell his numbers as do some religions today. Knowing of and loving our Savior, without knowing that the antichrist arrives first claiming to be Christ, is the very reason Christ said that He would become a stumbling block to those who possess the zeal to know Him but not the knowledge of His word.

While in your flesh body you need not fear anything physically from this want-to-be Christ. The real problem lies with your souls wellbeing. If for any reason you follow the antichrist, your soul automatically becomes mortal, which means it is liable to die. Your soul will still enter your eternal body, but you will have to spend 1,000 years away from Christ, in Paradise, unfortunately on the wrong side of the gulf with all, and I do mean all, and "all" that is implied. Those that do not overcome do however get a chance to see what they will miss for a long time. Like the rich man they also will burn with remorse. Remember, only satan and the fallen angels have already been sentenced to death. No one else will be sentenced to death (the second death) until the millennium is over and the Great White Throne Judgment takes place. FYI, the 7,000 fallen angels will be destroyed at the end of this earth age as recorded in Revelation 11:13. They will never be heard from again.

Satan, the old serpent from way back in the garden, will not be destroyed until after the millennium, and then only after he has had a chance to deceive, if he can, those patiently waiting on the wrong side of Paradise. It is not until this time that he and anyone now twice deceived go into the Lake of Fire where they are turned to ashes, blotted out. They and any memory of them are gone for Eternity. No one will burn in hell forever. What kind of heaven (Eternity) would it be if you knew that ole' Uncle Ned was doing the backstroke daily in the Lake of Fire? Our merciful Father would not allow this, either. Remember, Ned is one of God's children.

In light of full disclosure, I must tell you something now. You need to know God's warning toward those who do not take the time to study the letter, the *Bible*, which He wrote to us. He states in 2 Thessalonians verse 11 that He will give them strong delusions so that they might believe the lie that is the antichrist. In other words, if you want to believe a lie, God says, "I'll help you." I am not making this up. It sounds unfair I know, but Our Father has given us all the answers to the test, and He has already programmed us to know the true answer (truth) when we hear it, so it is fair.

Let's turn now to 2 Thessalonians with Paul as the author. 2 Thessalonians Chapter 2 describes in detail the events that will take place at the sixth trumpet and during the sixth vile. The subject of this chapter is set in the first verse. The subject being, "How do we gather back to Christ and when?" Paul's account parallels Mark 13 where we will be returning to soon.

2 Thessalonians 2:1. *"Now we beseech you, brethren, by* (about) *the coming of the Lord Jesus Christ, and by* (about) *our gathering together unto Him."*

Verse 2. *"That you be not soon shaken in mind, or be troubled, neither by spirit, nor by word, or letter from us, as that the day of Christ is at hand."*

Let me give you some background on this. Paul had written a letter prior to this, 1 Thessalonians, and some of the statements made in the letter caused confusion among the believers in Thessalonica. Paul, by His own admission, was rude in speech. Paul spoke colloquial Greek, or better stated, Street Greek. In plain English, Paul is difficult to understand, therefore many in Thessalonica who read the first letter were unintentionally led into believing that the second coming of Christ could happen at any moment. There are still many today who use this letter to teach the Rapture. A clear understanding of this subject was of such importance that Paul felt it necessary to clear the matter up and thus wrote the second letter to the Thessalonians. Stating with verse 3 of 2 Thessalonians.

"Let no man deceive you by any means: for that day shall not come, except (unless) *there come a falling away first, and that man (ish) be revealed, the son of perdition."*

"The son of perdition" is yet another name for the Antichrist. What Paul is saying here is do not listen to the traditions of man that make God's word void. You need to always check it out in God's word for yourself. Next, that man (ish) of sin, this is yet another name for antichrist, and a very fitting one at that. The son of perdition, this verse is redundant on purpose. It is for effect. Perdition means death. Satan has already been judged and sentenced to death in the Lake of Fire. He, upon his return, will literally be a dead man walking. Verse 4 says,

"Who opposeth and exalteth himself above all that is called God, or that is worshiped."

This is documentation that satan as antichrist will be claiming to be God, wanting mankind's worship and adulation.

"So that he as God sitteth in the temple of God, showing himself that he is God."

God's temple is on Mount Zion in Jerusalem. This is where Christ will sit for the millennium and then God Himself will rule from there for the Eternity. Now let's get back to Mark 13, (and let's pick it up with verse 5).

"And Jesus answering them began to say, take heed lest any man deceive you."

Any man, no matter what he is wearing. This includes me as well. Why?

"Thus saith the Lord; cursed be the man that trusteth in man."

Always check it out for yourself in Our Father's word. This is why I provide you with documentation. Mark 13:6.

"For many shall come in my name, saying, 'I am Christ,' and shall deceive many."

This translation is a little fuzzy. We are not just talking about the Jones town, Jim Jones, or the Waco City, David Kirresches that happen along once in a blue moon. It is talking about those who upon Christ's name claim to be teachers of His word, but instead do teach falsely. Some do this out of ignorance, while others have a more tainted agenda. God's word, many times, warns us of these wolves in sheep's clothing. You absolutely need to test their fruit. How? Again, In God's word, Mark 13:7.

"And when you shall hear of wars and rumors of wars, be not troubled; for such things must needs be: but the end shall not be yet."

Remember, the subject of Mark 13 is the end of this world age and the events that must take place to bring it to fruition. This particular verse is one that puzzles many, so let me clarify. What is the opposite of war? Peace! Antichrist will come in peacefully and prosperously claiming to be Christ, not as a violent, demonic horned monster, destroying any God-fearing individual that gets in his way. God always gives us types. When you hear platitudes such as peace, hope and socialism you can know we are getting close. Daniel 11:24.

"He (antichrist) *shall enter peaceably even upon the fattest places of the province* (US for example)*; he shall scatter among them* (those deceived) *the prey and the spoils, and riches."*

Antichrist will offer to pay off all your bills and debts if you will just worship him. He and his religious system (this is the second beast spoken of in Revelation) will usher in peace and prosperity.

The collapsed economy of the world will be restored and in an instant, all the world will be at peace. This is the beginning of the end. Pure genius isn't it? The headlines all over the world will most likely read 'Christ has returned.'

This will be the time the Elect will have to be on their toes. All of today's conflicts are in one way or another religiously motivated. Antichrist will be preaching peace and love for one another, and when he snaps his fingers and lightning bolts crash down at his command, or he levitates a car or heals a sick child, people who are not mentally prepared will follow him. Never forget that he has whatever power God allows him to have. If you are asking yourself why God would do this, the answer is to test those of us upon this earth. What is satan's motivation, you ask? Satan believes with every fiber in his supernatural body that if he can deceive enough, and thereby gather enough of God's children to worship him, God will have to bow down to him. How is that for arrogance? Satan believes God has a weakness exhibited by not destroying any souls, including satan himself, after the rebellion in the first earth age. Satan, in his arrogance, views this action as weak on God's part. In actuality, it was Our Father's infinite love for His children. Apparently satan is unaware that it is only due to his usefulness in God's overall plan to weed out the unfit for the Eternity that he is not already ashes. Our Father told us way back in Genesis that He will not change His mind.

I cannot for the life of me understand how satan can believe he will win when you factor in the millennium. During the millennium, satan is locked up, body and spirit, so he will have zero influence on those who did not overcome or were fooled in this age. Couple that with the fact that we will not be in flesh bodies in the millennium, and it does not look too good for satan. The following reasons are why I believe God's plan is perfect. Those who overcame in this age will in the millennium be able to cross over the gulf that separates paradise and teach those on the left side. Without any influence from satan and with no flesh nagging at them for attention, there will be more souls saved in the millennium than at any other time. Mark 13:8.

"For nation shall rise against nation and kingdom against kingdom: and there shall be earth quakes in divers (various) *places, and there shall be famines and troubles; these are the beginnings of the sorrows."*

The first part of this verse is a prophecy from Isaiah 19:2.

"Strife and violence within nations, brother against brother, and neighbor against neighbor."

Satan uses division to further his plan. One of the most obvious and disturbing examples of this can be seen in the religious denominations of the world today. Denominations in the Greek language means "division." Paul tells us in 1 Corinthians 11:18 that there are divisions in the church at Corinth and identifies the problem as being, some in the church feel they have a better connection with God then do the others. This proclivity is common in mankind and satan knows it. He is using it today. The fact that there are so many religious denominations is proof that he is winning. The wedges he has driven between Christians is blatantly clear. There is only one Christ yet so many divisions. A house divided cannot stand. These are the words of Jesus Christ. As far as natural disasters it is only going to get worse. Earthquakes and natural disasters are also happening at an ever-increasing rate and with inarguable intensity. Why? We are experiencing the birth pangs (sorrows) of Genesis 3:16. Famines are the famines prophesied in Amos 8:11. The hunger for hearing the truth. The sorrows of the end days have already begun, Mark 13:9.

"But take heed to yourselves; for they shall deliver you up to councils; and synagogues ye shall be beaten: and you shall be brought before rulers and kings for my sake, for a testimony against them."

This verse only applies to God's Elect. A select few of the Elect are called the 'Very Elect,' Matthew 24:24 states there are the "very Elect." Because of their steadfast refusal to worship the antichrist the very Elect will be called before the antichrist and many in his system to give a Holy Spirit inspired testimony. Only the Elect need be concerned about this, because the others who have been deceived will be living it up, playing church and enjoying the good life. One thing you must keep in mind is that to them you will be a blatant, defiant, atheist, because in their minds, they believe Jesus Christ is standing right in front of you. Mark 13:10 reads.

"And the Gospel must first be published among all nations."

Published in this context means broadcasted. The testimony of the Elect will be broadcasted throughout the whole world. The fulfillment of this prophesy would not have even been possible only a few short years ago. However, with the invention of the World Wide Web, it is possible to broadcast to every corner of the world. This prophesy's fulfillment is now possible, as we see in Mark 13:11. This verse documents that some will be called to give a testimony.

"But when they shall lead you and deliver you up, take no thought beforehand what you shall speak, neither do you premeditate. But whatsoever shall be given you in that hour, that speak ye: for it is not you that speak, but the Holy Spirit."

This is the only time that the unpardonable sin can be committed, and only one of God's Elect can commit it. This is obviously a very serious situation. The Elect (those who know the truth), when called before the antichrist, are not to speak their own mind, but rather allow the Holy Spirit (God's Spirit) to speak through them. Refusal to do so is unpardonable. Let's let Our Father's word explain it in Luke 12:8-12, Christ speaking.

Verse 8. *"Also I say to you, whosoever shall confess me before men, him shall the son of man* (Christ) *also confess before the angels of God.* Verse 9. *But he that denieth me before men shall be denied before the angels of God."*

Verse 10. "And whosoever shall speak a word against the son of man (Christ), *it shall be forgiven him: but unto them that blasphemy against the Holy Spirit, it shall not be forgiven."*

Verse 11. "And when they bring you unto the synagogues, and unto magistrates, and powers, take you no thought how or what thing you shall answer, or what you shall say."

Verse 12. "For the Holy Spirit shall teach (provide) *you in the same hour what you ought to say."*

There is a lot of information here, but let's boil it down. If, when delivered up before antichrist and his minions, an Elect refuses to allow the Holy Spirit to speak through him or her, it is an unforgivable sin. Verse 12 nails down the time frame. It is the hour of temptation, which occurs during the five-month tribulation. I do not believe that any Elect will commit this sin based on Matthew 24:24. Chapter 24 of the book of Matthew is a parallel chapter to Mark 13 and Luke 21. In Matthew 24:24, Christ Himself states regarding the testimony of the very Elect, *"Insomuch that, if it were possible they* (antichrist and his minions) *shall deceive even the very Elect."*

Deceive as it is used here means "to wear down to the point of breaking," thus the scorpion analogy. God's Elect will not bow a knee to antichrist! Mark 13:12 tells us,

"Now the brother shall betray the brother to death and the father, the son and children shall rise up against their parents, and shall cause them to be put to death."

This is a bad translation. Death, as it appears in this verse, should be read 'satan as antichrist.' Satan is death (spiritual death) to anyone who follows him. He is also the son of perdition, which again means death. The word 'to' in the manuscripts should be read 'before.' Reread this verse with those substitutions, and it will make more sense. Remember, satan as the Antichrist is claiming to be Christ. He is not about to blow his cover. 'Anti,' in the Greek language, means 'instead of. Staying with the subject, this verse is warning us that our own family members, those who have been deceived, will cause the Elect to be put (called up) before the antichrist. They, out of ignorance, will believe that leading you before the antichrist is the right thing to do. It may go something like this. Your family members have swallowed the antichrist bait. You have not. As prophesied, the antichrist has paid off all their debts, and they were substantial. Your family members are living the dream, worshiping and adoring antichrist's charisma and generosity. Life for them is perfect, but not for you. You are, in their eyes, an atheist and a rebel, but you are family, and they still love you. So, naturally, they want to help. They insist that you attend one of the many revivals that will no doubt be going on during that time. You go because the spirit moves you to do so, and let's face it, to also make the incessant badgering stop.

It is at this gathering when antichrist or one of his lieutenants (these will be the fallen angels) asks if there is anyone in the crowd who has someone with them who is not on board yet. They then will ask them to bring anyone up so that they can help them, you know, feel the love. This is a sort of alter call. You know what I am talking about, so you go up. After all, you figure this is the destiny of one of God's Elect. Well, being one of God's Elect, you will know what you are to do next. It is at this time that the Holy Spirit, the Spirit of God speaking through you, delivers a message that is so truthful and so powerful that many in the crowd have their spiritual eyes opened.

The blinders of deceit are removed by this testimony, and their view of this want-to-be Christ begins to change. Our Father always gives us types as examples. Where is there an example of this? In Acts 2:4. This is taking place on Pentecost day, soon after Christ ascended from the Mount of Olives.

"And they (the Apostles*) were filled with the Holy Spirit, and began to speak with other tongues, as the Spirit gave them utterance."*

Acts 2:5-6. *"And there were dwellings at Jerusalem Jews, devout men, under every nation under heaven. Now when this was noised abroad, the multitude came together, and were confounded, because every man heard them speak in his own language."*

This was not like some alter calls that go on today, where people speak gibberish that no one can understand. This Holy Spirit-delivered message was understood by all who were within earshot. This was a High Holy Day. There were people from all nations who spoke many different languages, and yet, all understood clearly the words the apostle spoke. Be very wary of traditions of men that dictate that you must speak in tongues, especially if it is unintelligible nonsense. The devil's spirit is allowed on this earth at this time, and his message is to confuse. This is not God's way, as declared in Corinthians 14:33.

"For God is not the author of Confusion."

Our Father loves his children. What loving father would mislead a child as it seeks the truth? None that I know. Do not ask me to document this, because I cannot, but I believe the language the apostles spoke will be the same language as the Very Elect will speak when they are called up to give a testimony. Mark 13:13 tells the Elect they won't be popular. Even among their own.

"And you shall be hated of all men for my name sake: but he that shall endure until the end, the same shall be saved."

This sounds pretty harsh, however, it makes perfect sense when you think about it. All the world will believe this fraud is the real Christ, when we have been warned that the antichrist comes first. That is next. Those deceived by satan, many perhaps, may not immediately turn back to the real Christ at the delivery of the Elect's Holy Spirit-inspired message, but over time they will. You will need to be prepared, because while in the process they may truly hate you. People do not like having their beliefs altered and certainly not at this level. If you do not follow the antichrist, be prepared to be very unpopular. Mark 13:14.

"But when you shall see the abomination of desolation, spoken of by Daniel the prophet, standing where it (he) *ought not* (let him that readeth understand) *then let them that be in Judea flee to the mountains."*

The abomination of desolation is the antichrist, documented in Daniel 11:31 and also in Revelation 13:13-14. In the above verse the reader should insert (he) for 'it.' Why? We have already established that antichrist is a man, not a condition. He, she, it in the Hebrew language all have the same value in a sentence. It is the subject that determines the value. The subject in this verse is antichrist, and he is a man (ish). Let's look at Mark 13:15.

"And let he that is on the house top not go down into the house, neither enter there in and take anything out of his house."

Do not take anything out of the house. Why? You will not have time (1 Corinthians 15:50-52). When Christ returns, in an instant, in the blink of an eye, all who are alive on this earth are changed into their celestial bodies. You will not need a change of clothes, either. You are going back to your celestial body. What will we wear in the millennium? (Revelation 14:13 tells us that the only thing you can take with you to heaven are your good works. They weave your garments in heaven (Revelation16:15). Furthermore, Mark 13:16 states,

"And let him that is in the field not turn back again for to take up his garment."

Again, you are not going to have time to get it, and you simply will not need it, which we can read in Mark 13:17.

"But woe to them that are with child and to them who give suck in those days."

This is one of those verses that is very often avoided by men of the cloth. Some will take a stab at it, but most avoid it altogether. Giving birth and motherhood, although challenging at times, are always a blessing. So many misinterpret this verse, because Christ is speaking spiritually here, as in your soul and your spiritual being. This verse is metaphorical and does not apply to only women – its warning is for men as well. What Christ is saying here is, 'when I come back, do not let me find you spiritually seduced (as in your mind) by satan (antichrist) and worse, nursing (helping) his deceitful religious system along. The second beast mentioned in the book of Revelation is a religious movement, and antichrist will be its leader. In 2 Corinthians 11:2-3 Paul writes,

"For I am jealous over you with godly jealously: for I have espoused you to one husband, that I may present you as a chaste virgin to Christ. But I fear, lest by any means, as the serpent beguiled Eve through his subtlety, so your minds should be corrupted from the simplicity that is Christ."

God's word uses the analogy that we are all espoused (engaged) to Christ for the Great White Wedding that is to take place when He returns at the Second Advent, at the end of this earth age. Imagine this – Christ returns after 2,000 years to find you have been spiritually (mindfully) seduced (deceived) by satan. Using the vernacular, you have been in bed with the devil and are spiritually impregnated (with lies) by him. Christ is going to be disappointed. Not only have you been impregnated (deceived) by his lies, but you are nursing (helping his deceitful system) along. Example: Causing a non-believing family member to be called up before him. There is an Old Testament verse that you can now read correctly, which is Isaiah 54:1.

"Sing (be happy), *o barren* (one), *thou that dist not bear; break forth into singing, and cry aloud, that thou dist not travail* (deliver) *with child: for are more the children of the desolate* (deceived) *than the children of the married wife.* (Christ) *Saith the Lord."*

This verse reinforces the fact that many more will be in bed with the antichrist than will wait for Christ. It would be better to never have had children at all, than to watch them go to their spiritual death. Thank God for the millennium. Mark 13:18 reads,

"And pray that your flight be not in winter."

The parable of the tares tells us that God's children are the wheat and the children of satan are the chaff or waste. When is harvest time for wheat? Summer, not winter. Christ is telling us not to be harvested early or out of season. This verse is a warning to us not to be deceived by satan when he appears first or out of season. Winter comes before summer. A parallel verse to the above verse is found in Matthew 24:40.

"*Then shall two be in the field, one shall be taken* (early) *and the other left* (behind)."

Two are working in a wheat field. The one left behind knows that the antichrist comes first and is not deceived and remains working in the field. He remains behind working and spreading the truth as God commanded. Mark 13:19 states.

"For in those days there shall be affliction, such was not from the beginning of creation which God created unto this time, neither shall be."

This earth age is the one and only time we will ever have to go through this, and thank God for that. Things may get a little rough, but only for those who do not follow antichrist, and remember the tribulation has been shortened by Christ Himself. Those who follow the antichrist will have it made and will be living it up. Those of us who hold out for the real Christ will experience a few bumps. We know from the Book of Luke Ch. 10 that they cannot touch one hair on our heads. That being said, you will be unpopular. It is quite likely we will not be able to buy or sell, so it is a good idea to have something you can trade. You can work for pay, and you can surely cash your social security checks. You can pretty much do anything as long as it does not require you to worship the beast, the one-world religious system. This you must not do! Never fear, God is in control at all times, and He always takes care of His own, according to Mark 13:20.

"And except that the Lord had shortened those days, no flesh should be saved: But for the Elect's sake, whom He has chosen (from the first earth age) *He hath shortened those days."*

For the Elect, His chosen.

This is some of the best news since Redemption itself! The time being shortened here is the time of the Tribulation. The Tribulation is the period of time, formerly seven years, which was shortened by Christ to five months. This is when satan and the fallen angels will be on this earth in an attempt to deceive (test) as many of God's children as will follow them.

Never forget that throughout the Tribulation, God is in control, and He promises never to tempt or test you beyond what you are able to handle, thus the shortened time of the Tribulation. Stay with God, and He will surely stay with you.

The truth of the matter is that the above verse is really written directly to God's Elect. If at this time you are wondering if you are one of God's Elect, the answer is this: If you know the truth about the antichrist and have compassion, you surely are one of Our Father's chosen. With that thought in mind, remember the others. The billions who are deceived by the antichrist will be living it up. With all their bills paid off, they have blind faith that all their infirmities will be healed by this so-called messiah. They will believe they have made it to the Eternity. This is why I say that if you are in your flesh body, it is not the True Christ. Never, ever forget this advice.

In light of full disclosure, I have to tell you that I have not been totally truthful to this point. I have not lied, but I have withheld some pertinent information so you will not worry any longer than necessary. Satan and his fallen angels are in fact cast out of heaven at the same time. They have only five months to operate, shortened from seven years. Now, this is the rest of the story.....

Satan as the antichrist was always prophesied to rise up in the middle of the Tribulation. In the Book of Daniel, it was referred to as a week (7) of years, no doubt distinguishing a time difference between our time and God's. Since Christ shortened satan's allotted time as the antichrist, he will now have only two and one half months (shortened from three and a half years) to accomplish his objective directly. He will wait out of sight until the fallen angels have had their two and one half months as leaders, to ramp up the already fevered pitch of today's religious wars in tandem with global one-worldism. This period between the arrivals of the fallen angels until satan saves the day will be tough, perhaps very rough for those who are not deceived. Let me make this perfectly clear. Satan will arrive with the fallen angels. It is in the middle of the five months that satan will rise from among the people (seas) and claim to be Christ, calming down the never-before-seen violence. It is then that those who believe He is Christ will have it made.

There will no doubt be skeptics. However, when standing in the temple in Jerusalem (where he should not be) speaking to the whole world via satellite, the antichrist will proceed to snap his fingers and on his command, lightning bolts from the heavens will crash to the earth and, trust me, all observing will believe he is

Christ returned.

You have to admit that it is perfect. Man, since the beginning of this age, has always attempted to control his fellow man. Today, considering his global abilities, this perverse dream is almost within his grasp. This flesh age, in my opinion, is a shortened version of the first earth age. Man, is man. Today's population has become somewhat calloused with a been-there-done-that attitude, because there is nothing New under the eternal sun.

So, what has not been done before? You may have guessed it. Only by divine/supernatural intervention could the world we live in today unite on anything. I am not talking about an alien invasion. There is nothing alien or unknown to Our Father. If UFO's exist, God knows about them. Our Fathers word does speak of metallic vehicles. Read the first chapter in the book of Ezekiel with your blinders off. If you do read it, keep a few points in mind. Ezekiel is being visited by God and is describing God's vehicles. No, God does not need a vehicle. However, He has His throne (it has mass) with Him, and, yes, there are souls (eyes) on board and Ezekiel can see them through the "rings" (rings means "rounded," like windows) Ezekiel 1:18. Verse 7 of this chapter describes these vehicles landing gear (feet) as calves' feet and their legs had no joints, they were straight. Imagine the lunar modules landing gear. In the last part of this verse Ezekiel describes the color of these vehicles as "burnished brass." The manuscripts say "highly polished bronze" as with verse 4. Verse 9 tells us they did not look where they went as would a donkey, these vehicles went up, down and sideways with ease. There is more than one vehicle and they are in formation around God's vehicle. In verse 12 spirit = people, *"Absent from this body is present with our Lord."* Verse 13 describes "fire" propulsion. Verse 16 tells us they look like a wheel within a wheel and these wheels were on their sides (horizontal) not (vertical) as on an ox cart. God loved Ezekiel so much that He visited him in person. Ezekiel 11:22 describes these vehicles leaving. The year is 513 B.C. And all he has seen at this point is an ox cart so I feel he did a great job describing these vehicles.

Look, this is one reason why in the process of exposing the

antichrist, we started way back in the first earth age and why I made the statement: "You have to understand what happened in the beginning to ever hope to understand the end."

Throughout this journey, by using God's word, we have discovered that there was a first earth age. We also discovered what the real sin in the garden was and learned that a supernatural (more natural) being created in the first earth age is in fact capable of impregnating a flesh woman. In chapter four of our journey, along come the fallen angels, and using God's word, we discovered that these supernatural beings again got at flesh women, and children were born of them, and the result was giants.

We were even shown the reason for their intrusions. All influxes were an attempt to pollute the line through which Jesus Christ would come, thus foiling God's plan of salvation, with the end result being satan saving his own doomed skin. It has been a process in which all events have been documented using God's letter, the Bible, our Father wrote to us. The fact is that satan and the fallen angels have enough mass to impregnate women, so they obviously need transportation. It is not that complicated. Go and stand (legally and safely) near the end of an airport runway, watch and think about it. Watch as these vehicles taxi and as they take off and land as soft as a dove. One last thought, when reading the Bible you come across the expression "chariots of fire", this is in reference to vehicles. "Chariot" means "to ride." Whirlwinds are from these vehicles as well.

God using satan and the fallen angels is about to double down. If there is a down side to God's plan, it is that even those who do not know the truth will have it rough for at least a portion of the Tribulation. It will be for three and one half months before antichrist rises. Just as it is today, so it will be then. Your geographical location will determine how badly and for how long you will experience this part of the Tribulation. On that subject, try to convince the Christians living in the Middle East today they are not already in the Tribulation. All I will say is that it will get worse, as documented in Matthew 24:21.

"There will be oppression not since the beginning of the world. Everyone will be primed to take the antichrist's bait."

The word tribulation during antichrist's reign, when applied to those who are deceived, by its very definition is as fraudulent as the antichrist himself. Tribulation means 'great distress or suffering caused by oppression.' Those who follow the antichrist will not experience this at all. God does not make mistakes, so did Our Father see this coming? Yes. Isaiah 29:16 states,

"Surely you are turning of things upside down." (In the end times).

Wrong is right and right is wrong. This prophesy is so very true and being fulfilled today. Just take a look around you, and look at this once great country. Those who do work labor for our servant government and not the other way around as it was intended to be. This is not unique to America – it is worldwide. The prophesy of Isaiah 29:16) is being fulfilled at this moment.

A one-world government is the first metaphorical beast spoken of in Revelation, the second beast being the one-world religious system headed by antichrist. As people get more and more conditioned, and therefore comfortable with surrendering their God-given right that is self-reliance, they will not hesitate to gravitate to the free ride the antichrist will offer when the one-world government attempt fails.

Yes, mankind's attempt at a one world government will fail. It is written that this (beast) system gets a deadly wound that antichrist heals with his religious system. This one world system exists today and is growing like a "beast." Uninformed people will be as dependent as misguided sheep to his spiritual slaughter. In speaking of prophesy being fulfilled, it is getting pretty tough to be a Christian in this country these days.

Then consider what is going on in the Middle East. Muslims are murdering Christians by the hundreds of thousands all in the name of religion. This kind of behavior is a type. Satan as antichrist, although physically peaceful, will be murdering souls by the billions. You must understand that this spiritual death is final. This is why I said that I do not believe there will be a nuclear holocaust. Again, why? Upon the real Christ's return, we are going to live on this earth for the 1,000 years of the millennium. If there were to be a nuclear holocaust, this earth would be uninhabitable. The billions mentioned in the Book of Revelation who die, suffer a mortal wound to their soul, not a physical death as so many believe. Do not misunderstand me – many will die a flesh death as a result of violence during the end times, but the vast majority will fall to satan's flood of lies.

I need to say at this time that I do not believe satan's religious movement will be a "religion" at all. I am talking about major denominations such as, Islam, or Catholicism. Denomination translated from the Hebrew language means "division." There is no fixing that. I believe he will preach Christianity, so be alert. After all, Christianity is not a religion – it is a reality. He will surely come when the world is in chaos.

Satan still retains all the knowledge from the first earth age. He is fully aware that God's children are programmed to recognize His truth when they hear it. Thus, he is going to mix truth with lies in an attempt to get their attention and then mislead them. If you do not know Our Father's word or at least that this man (ish) is a fake, you will be in a world of hurt for sure.

Very soon, emotions fueled by religious ideology all around the world are going to rise to a fevered pitch. It will be at this time that the fallen angels will arrive to fan the coals of violence that will lead the whole world to cry, "Peace, peace, peace!" This will be the time satan as the antichrist, having been waiting in the background, will rear his ugly head and bring about world peace; peacefully and prosperously, I must add. Satan is the quintessential narcissist, and we have documented that he believes he is better than God. The battle between Our Father and satan has been going on for thousands upon thousands of years, all the way back into the first earth age.

Satan and his angels have already been loosed in heaven, and a battle is taking place there at this moment. Very shortly, God's army, led by Michael, will cast this bunch out of heaven, that dimension. It is at this time that God's word says,

"Woe to those of us on this earth."

Now it is game-on for the Elect. If you are one of God's Elect, you must know the truth that we just exposed and seal it in your mind. It will take supernatural intervention to bring about WW III, just a little help from above, and it will take supernatural intervention to bring the perception of world peace. As with 9/11, neither man nor Hollywood has figured it out yet, and it is right there in the Bible. Not knowing that there was a first earth age is what keeps the blinders on. It is a sure bet that God's Elect will be able to identify the false christ when he arrives. I personally am expecting a very grandiose arrival, not some sneak attack. At the height of the violence, Revelation 13:1 states that.

"The antichrist shall rise up out of the sea."

At face value, this explains the depictions showing him to be a sea monster. That is just not true. The Book of Revelation is full of symbolism. This is why in Chapter 17 of this Book, the Angel of the Lord interprets certain things for John. He explains that the seas and waters as used in Revelation prophesy are, in fact, people and nations as we see in Revelation 17:15.

"And He saith to me (John)*, the waters* (seas) *that thou sawest, where the whore sitteth, are peoples, and multitudes, and nations, and tongues."*

The word "sitteth" indicates submission. The people of the world will worship this fake. We know that the whore spoken of in this verse is the antichrist and his one-world religious system that causes those betrothed (engaged) to Christ to whore after the false christ. I believe the Elect should be looking out for something more on the order of headlines reading 'Jesus Christ Returns!' This is when the short-lived party for the deceived begins, and the Tribulation shifts gears for the Elect.

Allow me to take it to a deeper level. Let us take some time and document that Christ has shortened the Tribulation to five months. Your proof is found in the Book of Revelation, Chapter Nine. The subject of this chapter includes the antichrist, his fallen angels, and the already swarming locust army. These verses will reveal to us how they will treat the Elect as well. There are a few metaphors and some symbolism used in this chapter that will need clarification. We will do it as we go. Revelation 9:1 says,

"The fifth angel sounded and I saw a star fall from heaven unto the earth: and to him (satan) *was given the key to the bottomless pit."*

What is being said here is that satan has arrived and is now in control. Keep in mind that he remains behind the scene, yet he is controlling his angels. Although this event is yet future, Christ did speak of it when He was still on this earth in Luke 10:18.

"And He (Christ) *said unto them, 'I beheld satan as lightening fall from heaven'."*

Christ was predicting the event of Revelation 9:1 more than 2,000 years ago. It is going to happen. This verse may be a bit of a digression, but it is important that you always remember this promise from Our Father, when He was yet in a flesh body. It is the next verse in Luke anyway, specifically, in Luke 10:19.

"Behold, I give you power to tread on serpents and scorpions, and over all the power of the enemy."

"Nothing shall by any means hurt you." We have this power

every day, but never as much as when, very soon, you will be looking this enemy directly in the eye. Continuing to prove that the Tribulation is only five months, we read Revelation 9:2.

"And he (Michael) *opened the bottomless pit; and there arose a smoke out of the pit, as the smoke of a great furnace; and the sun and the air were darkened by reason of the smoke."*

Satan and the fallen angels are released from the pit, and all are on their way to this earth. Woe to us on earth. The fallen angels will become leaders in the already warring (look at the Middle East today) locust army on this earth. Locust in the Hebrew language is "arabh," which translates to Arab in English. The locust army spoken of in Joel Chapter 2 is already swarming in the world today. Locusts is a metaphor helping to describe this army's massive numbers and their intent to strip and devour souls.

The fallen angels will become leaders in the earth's already swarming locust army, as well as any other conflicts they can ramp up to prime the pump for antichrist's magic show. When the fallen angels take over as leaders, the religious unrest, and any unrest for that matter that you see today, is destined to hit a crescendo. We already know where satan will be during that time. He is in the shadows waiting to save the day by calming everything down. It will appear to most that he comes out of nowhere. The already escalating conflicts existing on earth today will, with supernatural intervention, get so bad that the whole world will be crying for peace. Revelation 9:3 tells us,

"And there came out of the smoke locusts upon the earth; and unto them was given power, as the scorpions of the earth have power."

We know of the metaphor of the scorpion turning its victim's backbone to mush and that this is how the Antichrist and his, will work to wear down the Elect. The vast majority of the world will bow immediately to the antichrist when he rises up, but the Elect will not. They and the two witnesses will be testifying in an attempt to expose this fraud. They are aware that while antichrist is speaking great promises and platitudes to the masses, while behind the scenes he attends to his sinister agenda. Toward the end of his two and a half month reign, he will be growing increasingly impatient. By now he will truly be feeling the effects of the two witnesses and the Elects' testimonies. Being a narcissist he feels only he can carry out the plan. However, he is very aware of God's command in Revelation 9:4 below.

"*And it was commanded them* (satan and the fallen angels only) *that they should not hurt the grass* (Elect) *of the earth, neither any green thing, neither any tree; bet only those men* (mankind) *which have not the seal of God in their foreheads*."

This verse needs some explanation. Let's do the last part of this verse first. The seal of God is knowing the truth about satan's plan. The Elect must have this truth sealed in their foreheads. What is in your forehead? Your brain. "Grass", "green thing", and "tree" represent living things (spiritually.) These are metaphors for God's Elect. Because God's Elect cannot be fooled by antichrist, their souls are and will remain spiritually alive. Anyone who is deceived by antichrist is fair game, and for as long as they are deceived, their souls are mortal; which means 'liable to die.' We are not talking physically at this time. Satan has been commanded by God not to touch one hair on the heads of the Elect, and satan has passed this order down the chain of command. That being said, we know this order will be disobeyed when they kill the two witnesses in Jerusalem. This action brings their fun to an end. Remember, we have covered it – those deceived will be partying and exchanging gifts since the death of these two men of the Living God.

This war, World War III if you want, is being fought over religious beliefs. The fallen angels can direct, but they cannot have a direct hand in any physical violence. Their job is to fan the coals. The locust army's mantra is 'convert or die,' and satan and his fallen angels know they have but a short time. The next verse is very important, and the reason we came to this chapter of Revelation. Revelation 9:5.

"And to them (satan and the fallen angels) *it was given that they should not kill them* (the Elect)*, but that they should be tormented* (the Elect) *five months: and their torment was as the torment of a scorpion, when he* (it) *striketh a man."*

FYI: This verse is another case where there is a wrong translation of the word 'he' (remember he, she, it), no big deal. Scorpions are (its) not men. The fallen angels look like men (ish), but only act as scorpions. Here we have the scorpion analogy again. They cannot touch one hair on the heads of God's Elect. They will be able to brow beat them as well as torment them with lies. And do not forget, your deceived family members will be beating on you, also.

If you want to read the entire version of the Tribulation and the events for yourself, it can be found in the Book of Daniel Chapter 11 starting with verse 20. In verse 21 'vile person' is another name for antichrist. Keep in mind that this is the seven-year version. Christ shortened the time after Daniel's prophesies. God will somehow accelerate this process and accomplish it in five months. Five in biblical numerics means 'grace.'

There you have it in God's own words! Satan, the fallen angels and the locust army have only five months in which to torment and deceive as many of God's children as they can. This will be long enough, believe me! Something to keep in mind is that the season of the locust in Jerusalem (our barometer) is a five-month period, May through September. Why is Jerusalem his target? Satan is the great imitator, and Jerusalem is where God will place His throne for the Eternity. Your documentation is in the same book we are reading from now.

I have not given the event that we are going to talk about next nearly enough attention, so I will now. The apocalypse is now the elephant in the room. It has been on your mind, so what does the Bible say about it?

The word apocalypse does not appear anywhere in the Bible. Webster's dictionary gives a definition that states, 'a cataclysm in which evil forces are destroyed.' Webster pretty much nails it. There are not too many people who do not believe the apocalypse will be the last great cataclysmic event that will end mankind forever. That is just not how it happens, as we will discover.

Before we go any further with the apocalypse, there is another word whose definition is applicable at this time. That word is 'Apostasy,' also not found in the Bible. It means 'abandonment of a former loyalty for another.' Although this word is not found in the *Bible*, its implication certainly is. We just covered it. When the antichrist arrives, billions will give up their love for Jesus Christ and out of ignorance, worship (love) the antichrist. This transition is called 'The Great Apostasy,' and it happens just prior to the apocalypse.

The apocalypse occurs at the end of the five-month Tribulation just before the real Christ returns with his army and defeats the antichrist and his army (the enemy). Mankind (God's children) are not the real enemy in God's eyes. Satan and the fallen angels are. All God's children who came through this age in flesh go into the millennium. At the apocalypse, we do not fire a shot. In an instant, in the twinkling of an eye, all knees will bow at the sight of the real Jesus Christ, and then the millennium begins. The apocalypse is good news for those who did not worship the antichrist. Hang tough. It is written. It will happen, Back to Mark 13:21.

"And then if any man shall say to you, 'Lo here is Christ, or, lo he is here,' believe them not."

Remember, we read in Revelation 13:8 that the whole world will be deceived, with the exception of those with the truth sealed, immovable in their foreheads, the Elect. Antichrist is coming at the sixth trump. Just remember this. If you are in your flesh body, it is not Christ. "Christ comes at the 7th and last trump." Then in an instant we are all changed into our eternal bodies. If someone tells you Christ has returned, pinch yourself. If it hurts, it is not

Christ. Hang tough and wait, which we are reminded to do in Mark 13:22.

"For false Christs and false prophets shall rise and shall show signs and wonders, to seduce, if it were possible, even the Elect."

Take note of the word "shall." It is going to happen. We have documented that wonders are miracles. Revelation 13:13-14.

"The Elect will have their work cut out for them, but they will not fail."

Why? They have a destiny to fulfill. In Ephesians 1-4 and Romans 8:29-30, Christ warned us that there will be false prophets in this flesh age, specifically in Ezekiel 13:1-8. Christ instructs us to "Test their fruit." and not take what they say at face value. Check out what they teach in God's Word. Mark 13:20.

"But take heed: Behold I have foretold you all things."

The Bible is Our Father's way of communicating to us in this flesh age. Amos 3:7 states.

"Surely the Lord God will do nothing, unless He revealed His secret unto His servants, the prophets. And they unto us through teachers."

There are no mysteries in Our Father's word, just those who are ignorant in it. It is my hope that by having read this book, you will have gained knowledge as well as a desire to read Our Father's book. When God sees one of His children with His book open searching for answers, it truly makes His day. When you make His day, He is going to make yours, with blessings. This age is nearly at the end. Knowledge in God's word will assure your place with Him in the Eternity. Mark 13:24 declares the following.

"But in those days, after the tribulation, the sun shall be darkened and the moon shall not give her light."

After the Tribulation, Christ has just returned, and we are in our angelic bodies. This is the beginning of the millennium, 1,000 years of teaching. Christ is here with us on earth, and His light is the light of life. Truth. The moon, the stars and even the sun's light will pale to the light of the world. Take note, the Tribulation is over and we are still around. We are here on this earth. Why? No one has flown away! Mark 13:25 states,

"And the stars of Heaven shall fall, and the powers that are in Heaven shall be shaken."

This documents that heaven also will be shaken. Think of heaven as another dimension. There is war in heaven at this time (Revelation 12:7). Heaven will be on this earth for the Eternity. How can we be sure? The definition of heaven is wherever God is. Revelation 21:1-4.

"And I (John) *saw a New heaven and a New earth: for the former heaven and the former earth were passed away; and there was no more sea. And I saw the holy city, New Jerusalem, coming down from God out of heaven, prepared as a bride adorned for her New husband. And I heard a great voice out of heaven saying, 'behold, the tabernacle of God is with men, and he will dwell with them, and they shall be His people, and God Himself shall be with them* (Father, son, and Holy Spirit as on entity) *and be their God*'.
And God shall wipe away all tears from their eyes." "For, behold, I create New heavens and a New earth: and the former shall not be remembered, nor come to mind."

This answers the question as to whether we will recall experiences from this earth age. None at all.

Mark 13:26 *"And then shall they see the Son of Man coming in the clouds with great power and glory."*

This is at the sounding of the seventh trumpet. Christ returns to this earth, and instantly the millennium begins, as we are told in Mark 13:27. This dove tails with "the parable of the tares."

"And then shall He send His angels, and gather His Elect from the four winds, from the uttermost part of the earth to the upper most part of heaven."

This verse takes us full circle. We are back to the end of the parable of the tares. God at this time gathers all the wheat into His barn. Anything that offends is thrown into the Lake of Fire never to be heard from again. One more verse to end this chapter. The timing of this verse is just after Christ's feet have set down on the Mount of Olives and all have been changed into their angelic bodies and the dust from all who have run to meet Christ has settled. Isaiah 14:12-16.

"How art thou fallen from heaven, O lucifer, son of the morning! How art thou cut (cast) down to the ground, which dist weaken the nations!" (And caused all the trouble in this flesh age).

"For thou hast said in thy heart, I will ascend to heaven, I will exalt my throne above the stars of God (that's us, God's children): I (satan as antichrist) will also sit upon the Mount of Congregation (Mt. Zion), in the sides of (to) the north" (north side is where Christ's throne will be:

"I will ascend above the heights of the clouds; I will be like the Most High" (God).

"Yet thou shalt be brought down to hell (lake of fire)*, on the sides of the pit."*

"They that see thee shall narrowly look upon thee (us)*, and consider thee, saying, "IS THIS THE MAN"* (ish') *that made the earth to tremble, that did shake* (up) *the kingdoms;"*

There you have it. After Christ's feet have touched down at the seventh trumpet, all who are in their angelic bodies will look upon satan in a different light. He will look to us at that time like the little narcissistic lying weasel that he really is. Our flesh bodies pale in comparison to our angelic bodies and here is your proof.

Now the headlines will read, 'We Win! World War III is over!'

CHAPTER 8

THE RAPTURE, FACT OR FICTION?

The information contained in this chapter could save your soul. The facts that will be presented are not meant to offend anyone. They are meant only to inform. Everyone has to decide for themselves. Isaiah 48:16 tells us,

"I (God) have not spoken in secret from the beginning."

There is a nasty rumor circulating out there. The rumor is that anyone who is a saved Christian will, at the beginning of the Tribulation, be raptured out of here, never having to suffer the horrors they believe are inherent with it. This is one of those situations that if it sounds too good to be true, chances are it is not true. In the case of the rapture doctrine, it just is not true. It is not biblical. The rapture is simply a figment of man's, or more accurately stated, woman's Utopian imagination.

Now I have to agree, there are many who will say that the rapture theory, also known as the flyaway doctrine, is biblical. The word rapture does not appear anywhere in the Bible. A commonly offered defense is that the word 'trinity' in reference to The God Head, Father, Son and Holy Spirit, cannot be found in the Bible, either. This statement is correct, but they are comparing apples to oranges here. Speaking of apples, the rapture is as big a myth as is the fairy tale that Eve ate an apple in the Garden and this act of disobedience introduced sin into the world. While Eve's tale inhibits one from truly understanding the Bible, the rapture doctrine is far more damaging in that it plays right into satan's plan of deception and cost you your soul, as we have revealed. Belief in the rapture could ultimately cost you the Eternity. This is why it is such a very dangerous fable.

I do not know when or how the fairy tale in the Garden of Eden got its start, but the rapture theory's beginning is well documented. The year was 1830. A very sick (physically ill) woman, living in the small ship-building town of Port Glasgow, Scotland, dreamed it up, literally. Mary McDonald, while in and out of consciousness, awoke with a gasp and shared the dream she had experienced while comatose, with the two ministers at her bedside. These men of the cloth liked what they heard, and they ran with it. A short two years later in 1832, this ill-founded revelation began to get some traction. Well, the rest, as they say, is history. I am going to present the facts. Whether you believe them is a choice that you, with the help of your Heavenly Father, will have to make.

That being said let me explain the "Rapture theory." This theory is the belief that anyone that is "saved" will fly from this earth thus escaping the Great Tribulation. This also includes those in their graves. Both will fly out of here like birds just before the tribulation of the antichrist. There are a few problems with this belief scripturally and when you apply common sense. Why would Our Father have given us all the prophesy regarding the end time (what you have just read) if you are going to be out of here anyway. God does not waste time. Second, if anyone deserves to be out of here it is God's Elect, after all they stood with Him during satan's rebellion in the first earth age. The Elect aren't going anywhere, they are going to be here to give a testimony as scripture states. It is written in God's word and will happen as written. Remember the rule of thumb. If it does not make sense it is not God's word. Besides, Paul tells us in 2 Corinthians Ch. 5 verse 6-7 that when we are absent (deceased) from these flesh bodies we go instantly to our Father from where they came from, i.e. the first earth age. Ecclesiastes 12:6-7 is further documentation. No one is going to fly out of their grave because no one is in there. They are "home" with Our Lord.

"God is not the God of the dead, but of the living."

We are told in Ephesians 6:11:11-17 that we are to put on the Gospel armor. Why armor up if you are going to be out of here. Again, it does not make sense. Verse 13 of Ephesians lets us know the time frame *"the evil day"* to apply this Godly advice.

"Wherefore take unto you the whole armor of God, that you may be able to withstand in "the evil day," and having done all, to stand."

"The evil day" is referring to the tribulation.

Why am I so concerned about the rapture theory? Here is the reason. If you are a believer in the rapture then you believe that Christ will come next to rapture you out of here. As has been covered in depth in the chapters of this book satan is coming back next claiming to be Jesus Christ. Can you see a problem? If you believe that Christ is coming next to rapture you out of here, as satan performs miracles, you will be deceived. You will worship him when he claims he will fly you out of here. We have covered their vehicles. Maybe he will say there is an asteroid headed at the earth and you must evacuate. I do not know. What I do know is he will be supernatural and therefore an illusionist. I have never said that staying put and waiting on the real Christ would be easy.

Let's look at some scripture that is used to support the rapture theory. Confusion concerning this matter is the primary reason Paul wrote the second letter to the Thessalonians. It had gotten back to Paul that there was much confusion concerning his first letters references to events at the end of this flesh age. The believers at Thessalonica, from this letter, got the idea that the end of the world could come for them at any moment, thus another name for the rapture, the "any moment doctrine," as it is called today. Paul, noting the gravity of the situation, responded quickly with a second letter its intent being to clear up any confusion on the matter. This is why Paul, in the first two verses of Chapter Two in his second letter to the Thessalonians, apologizes.

This also explains the letters' brief and succinct message.

Now God's word tells us that when it comes to the end days, He has told us everything we need to know. It then begs the question: Did He foresee the Rapture rumor coming? The answer is, "Yes." The Book of Ezekiel Chapter 13 holds some of the answers to debunking this dangerous belief. However, before we go there, let us look at some scripture rapture believers use to document their theory. It is a sure bet any rapture believer will lead you to, 1 Thessalonians 4:16.

"For the Lord Himself shall descend from heaven with a shout, with the voice of the archangel, and with the trump (trumpet) *of God: and the dead in Christ shall rise first."*

The first part of this verse is correct. Christ will descend from above (as He ascended in Acts 1:9-11), His feet touching down on the Mount of Olives at the sounding of the seventh trumpet as Michael cries out victory. It is the last statement of 1 Thessalonians 4:16 that is so misunderstood. *'The dead in Christ shall rise first.'* Why? They are already gone! Absent from this flesh body is to be instantly with the Lord in heaven, (that dimension). This is the problem with not identifying the subject first. In this case you have to back up to verse 13 of Ch.4 to pick up the subject which is "where are the dead?" No one who has died, and by whatever means, is out there in some hole in the ground. They are with the Lord. All that remains of them, depending on how long they have been dead, is a skeleton or a talcum powder-like dust. God, Our Father, is not the Father of the dead, He is the Father of the living, whether in a flesh body or a celestial body. No one will fly out of the graves, because none of God's children are in them. Anyone with children, if they had God's power, would not allow their child to lay in a cold, dark, dank hole. 1 Thessalonians 4:17 goes on to explain,

"Then we which are alive, and remain, shall be caught up together with them in the clouds, to meet the Lord in the air: and

so shall we ever be with the Lord. "

"We which are alive and remain." Take this statement back to 1 Corinthians 15:51-52. *"In an instant, in the twinkling of an eye."*

Those of us who are on this earth at the instant Christ returns are in that same instant changed into our other bodies. It is my heartfelt belief that, unbeknownst to Paul, these verses were written to us, as we are living in the end days that are the subject of this verse. Why Paul in 1 Corinthians 10:11 tells us the lessons of the Bible, both Old and New Testaments, are for those of us in these end times.

The fly away believers have to totally ignore Acts Chapter 1 as well as 2 Thessalonians in order to arrive at and defend their interpretation of 1 Thessalonians 4:16 & 17. It is at best a long shot and at worst an opening of a door to those who would argue that the Bible contradicts itself. From the beginning of this book, I have stressed the importance of identifying the subject to make an accurate interpretation of the meaning in the verses that follow.

With that in mind, let's pick up the subject of 1 Thessalonians 4:16 & 17 and then read the verses the way Our Father would have them read. Keep in mind that later we are going to the Book of Ezekiel and document that Our Father knew this false doctrine would manifest itself at some point in time. Let's back up to 1 Thessalonians 4:13. This verse sets the subject, and when God sets the subject, no man has license to change its meaning, Verse 13.

"But I would not have you be ignorant, brethern, concerning them which are asleep (dead), *that you sorrow not, even as others which have no hope."*

Notice the use of the word "ignorant." Paul is not mincing words here. This is important, and because you now know satan's plan, you can see why it is so important. 'Asleep' in the Greek language is 'kekoiummevcov.' It simply means 'dead.' "Those who have no hope" are the ignorant who believe that the dead are in some hole in the ground or at the bottom of the ocean. The subject of the above verse is, 'Where are the dead?' Read 1 Thessalonians starting with verse 13 with this subject in mind and read it to verse 18. Paul does not want us to be ignorant of this fact and is about to explain in 1 Thessalonians 4:14.

"For if we believe that Jesus died and rose again, even so them also who sleep in Jesus will God bring with Him."

Here we go! The first statement of this verse: If you do not believe that Christ died and then three and one half days later arose from the grave, then quite simply, you are not a Christian. So, of course you believe, or you would not be reading this book and certainly not this far into it. Furthermore, it is written that Christ will return with His army made up of those who overcame in this flesh age and have passed on (those on the right side of Paradise only, the others do not get the privilege). Therefore, it stands to reason that if Christ brings once flesh beings (now called angels) with Him, they have to be with Him, and according to 2 Corinthians 5:6-7, they are. Again, they are not in some hole in the ground waiting to fly up and meet them half way, they are with Our Father at this very moment.

So what is Paul's message so far? Rejoice, not sorrow, for those who have shuffled off this mortal coil (died) and for whom the flesh test is complete. Christ is going to bring some of them with Him at the seventh trumpets' sounding. But for now, they are safe and at rest (peace) with our Lord. They are, in that dimension, going about their business. I cannot help but wonder what they think about us still here and if they even ponder it at all. My guess is that they are not all that worried. I mean, the worst that could happen is we die and join them. And besides, overcome or not, there is always the millennium to teach those who did not overcome. 1 Thessalonians 4:15 reads,

"For this we say unto you by the word of the Lord, that we which are alive and remain unto the coming of the Lord, shall not

prevent them which are asleep."

"Prevent" is an Old Saxon word that means to "precede" or go "before." Remember, when the King James was written in the year 1611, it was Shakespeare's time, and the language is difficult to understand. The manuscripts are crystal clear. They say that 'those who are alive will not go (to our Lord) before those who die.' Why? Those who have died are already gone! This is how Christ can bring them with Him when He returns. The rest of us alive on the earth are waiting for Christ to return at the 7th trumpet not the 6th. You can check me out in 1 Corinthians 15:51-52. It is just that simple.

Now let's read the next two verses, the verses that rapture believers use, and read them as they should be read, keeping the subject in focus. 2 Thessalonians 4:16.

"For the Lord Himself shall descend from heaven with a shout, with the voice of the Archangel, and with the trump of God: and the dead in Christ shall rise first."

"The dead shall rise first." Why? They are already gone and reside with The Lord. They are not going to fly out of the graves, because Christ is going to bring them with Him, as documented in 2 Thessalonians 4:17.

"Then we which are alive and remain (us), *shall be caught up* (led) *together with them* (those that Christ brings with Him when he returns), *in* (the) *clouds, to meet the Lord in the air* (Ruach)*: and so shall we ever be with the Lord."*

First eliminate 'the,' – it does not appear in the manuscripts. The clouds being referred to here are clouds of witnesses, believers, (those who did not worship the antichrist, for example). Because of the Elect's testimony there are going to be a swarm (great number) of them. Remember, Paul spoke Street Greek. So your proof that Paul is talking figuratively in the above verse and that he is in fact referring to clouds of people, can be found in Hebrews 12:1-2, Paul speaking.

"Wherefore seeing we are also compassed about with so great a cloud of witnesses let us lay aside every weight, and the sin which doth so easily beset us, and let us run with patience the race that is set before us."

Paul, several times uses the analogy of a foot race to illustrate a Christian's life, as a marathon runner practices discipline and restraint. Another example is found in 1 Corinthians 9:24-27.

"Know you not that they that run in a race, all run, but (only) *one receives the prize? So run that you may obtain* (it)."

Paul goes on in the verses that follow to explain that it takes practice, discipline and restraint to win the prize. In the case of a Christian, the prize is everlasting life. Paul was a free born Roman citizen (Acts 22:28) and no doubt a fan of the Olympics. I believe these examples should clarify the actual intent that Paul had in mind. Back to 1 Thessalonians 4:17 – let's look at the word 'air' as it is used in this verse. Air in the Greek language is ah-ayr, which means "Spirit." In the manuscripts the word is 'ruach' and means "the breath that is life." This is the same breath that God breathed into Adam way back in Genesis 2:7. Let me make this perfectly clear. The word 'air' as used in (verse 17 of I Thessalonians Ch. 4) does not mean atmosphere. The Greek word for atmosphere is pnuma, as in pneumatic air tools. Next, let's look at the phrase 'caught up' it should be read 'led.' Let us go ahead and read 1 Thessalonians 4:17 in plain English.

"Then those of us who are alive on this earth when Christ returns will be led along with those who Christ has chosen to bring with Him, in such large numbers that it will look like a swarm (cloud) *of bees and then we will be forever with Christ."*

I know that the original verses are sketchy at best. So did Paul. It confused those in Thessalonica so badly that Paul felt it necessary to write the second letter. Now let's go into why believing in the rapture theory or fly away doctrine can lead you to eternal damnation. There is another verse commonly used to prop up the rapture theory that lies in the Book of Revelation, in Revelation 3:10.

"Because thou hast kept the word of my patience, (you waited like I told you) *also will I keep you from the hour of temptation* (when satan deceives, the tribulation), *which shall come upon all the world to try them that dwell* (live) *upon the earth."*

The word "keep" as it is used here is 'ek' in the original Greek language. There are only two prepositions in the Greek language whose meanings are applicable in this case. First, you have to imagine a circle – draw one if you like and let it represent the earth. The first preposition that could be used in this application is 'apo,' which denotes motion from the surface of an object, as if you were to draw a line moving out from the circumference or outer surface of the circle into the air. However, Saint John specifically used the preposition 'ek,' which stands in direct contrast with 'apo' and denotes motion from the interior or center of a circle then moving out from there.

If Saint John were referring to the rapture, He would have certainly used apo in place of ek. This is not a mistake. Mankind does not live in the earth ek, we live on the earth, apo. So, what did Saint John have in mind when He wrote this verse? John knew that when satan returns, his one-world religious system would definitely be the center of everyone's attention. The message of Revelation 3:10 should read, God speaking.

"That because you searched, found and kept to My teachings, I will keep you away from or out of satan's circle of deception."

In other words, you know the truth and will not get involved with satan. Another verse that that rapturists use is found in the book of Matthew 24:20.

"But pray you that your flight be not in the winter, neither on the Sabbath day."

The subject of Matthew 24 is "when will the end be and what will be the signs?" This verse is a warning to those who believe they will fly away to save their souls. Think back to the "parable of the tares" we covered in a previous chapter. Remember God's children in the end are referred to as "Wheat." The end of this earth age is called the "harvest." When is harvest time for wheat? Summer not winter. Winter comes before summer. What Christ is saying in this verse is "Do not be harvested early" or out of season. You do not want to be taken first.

Staying with the "parable of the tares" let's look at yet another verse in Matthew that is often used to support the rapture. Matthew 24:40.

"Then shall two be in the field; the one shall be taken, and the other left" (Behind).

Again, the parable of the tares is your reference. "The field" we know is a wheat field. The one taken early has been raptured out. The one left behind remains as instructed, working in the field among the wheat. The wheat are God's children and this worker is an Elect. As an Elect he remains working (teaching) God's children throughout the tribulation, exposing the Antichrist as a fraud. Sit tight.

Lastly, let's go to the Book of Ezekiel and read for ourselves just what God has to say about the rapture and also how he feels about those who mislead his children by teaching it, as documented in Ezekiel 13:1.

"And the word of the Lord came unto me (Ezekiel) *saying."*

Furthermore, Ezekiel 13:2 states.

"Son of man, prophesy against the prophets (teachers) *of Israel (the tribes) that prophesy, and say unto them that prophesy but out of their own hearts."*

There you have it. The subject of this entire chapter is God's disdain toward false prophets, teachers or preachers. We have previously exposed satan's plan. He intends to come next at the sixth trumpet claiming to be Jesus Christ. He will be supernatural, which simply means more natural and capable of performing miracles in the site of every soul on this earth. Who is prepared for that? You are, if you have read this book. Being aware of the popularity of the fly-away doctrine, satan, as antichrist, will undoubtedly offer to fly you out of here. Why? I do not know. Satan is an illusionist, and he may convince them there is an asteroid headed at the earth or some other kind of apocalyptic disaster. The bottom line is he will attack at our weaknesses, our ignorance of God's word.

Win, lose or draw, if you believe that Christ comes next to remove you before the Tribulation, you will, out of ignorance, end up worshiping satan. In this case ignorance will not excuse you in God's eyes. Our Father has too many times and in too many places told us that the false christ comes first (next) at the sixth trumpet, and that Christ, the real Christ, does not appear until the seventh and last trumpet. Ponder this – God's Elect are going to be here during the Tribulation to deliver a Holy Spirit inspired message to those living on the earth and who are deceived by the antichrist. Many, many, many of the people deceived will be lifelong, God loving people. The Elect's message, inspired by the Holy Spirit, will ultimately make many of those deceived realize they are mistaken and turn them back to the real King of Kings. Remember, it is never too late to repent. Our Father gave us this example with the thief on the cross with Christ. There will be only two types of people on the earth at this time – the Elect who know the truth and those who are deceived by antichrist. The Elect are going to stay put. Tell me who is left who are worthy for God to take? Ezekiel 13:3 reads.

"Thus saith the Lord God; (listen up) *woe unto the foolish prophets, that follow their own spirit, and have seen nothing."*

This is directed at false preachers/teachers, etc. You know the type. In a display of one-upmanship they say, "I talked to God today and He said..." Our Father hates this kind of arrogance. He says He never talked to them and did not tell them what to say. Verse 4 states.

"O Israel, thy prophets (teachers/preachers), are like the foxes in the deserts."

This is an analogy. A comparison. The connection God wants the reader to make here is that these false preachers are sly (sneaky) like a fox. A fox is such a crafty animal that he is able to survive (make a living) when the food supply is very, very scarce. In this verse, the *foxes* are these false, for-profit-only preachers, who preach not God's word, but what they dream up in their own minds. They do it for personal gain in a time when food (the truth in God's word) is so very scarce. God goes on to chastise these false teachers in the next 12 verses, but we are going to skip down to Ezekiel 13:17 and get a first-hand view as to how Our Father feels about the false teaching of the rapture or fly-away doctrine.

"Likewise son of man, set thy face against the daughters (religions or churches) *of thy people, which prophesy out of their heart; and prophesy* (teach) *against them."*

God instructs Ezekiel to teach the truth to the people. And in verse 18.

"And say, thus saith the Lord God; Woe to the women (churches)

that sew pillows (coverings) *to all armholes* (hands), *and make kerchiefs upon the head of every stature to hunt souls* (remember the fox)! *Will you hunt the souls of my people* (children), *and will you save the souls alive that come to you?*

God is asking a question of these false teachers. First, only God can save a soul, not man – this is sarcasm on Our Father's part. Without being able to take this verse back to the original Hebrew, it would be impossible to understand. But with the aid of the Greens Interlinear and the Strong's Concordance, and studying under a scholar who has the ability to read and speak Hebrew and Greek, it is possible.

Let's break this verse way down. Women is a Hebraism for churches and religions. This is widely accepted. Pillows is 'kesathoth' in the Hebrew, #3704 in the Strong's Concordance. It means 'coverings'. Armholes = hands it is "atstsiyl," and is #679 in the Strong s Concordance. It means 'the joints or knuckles of the hand.' It is paired with the word "yad" #3027 in the Strong's Concordance, and it means an outstretched hand. Kerchiefs means veils, as in a veil that is used to cover the eyes. "Stature" means 'men of high stature,' i.e., religious leaders or, as in Christ's day, political leaders (many were one in the same at that time). History will repeat itself concerning this situation when the antichrist establishes his one-world religion that will transcend all governments. "To Hunt souls" these false preachers are more interested in increasing their memberships then they are in teaching the truth.

Let's face it, the fly-away doctrine sounds awful good and is a tantalizing bait. This is a classic example of how making a religion out of a few verses can do so much damage. I do not understand how any teacher worth his salt could claim to have read the Bible where there are so many examples against the Rapture and teach such a falsehood.

Keeping in mind that God is dressing down false teachers, this verse should read.

"And thus saith the Lord, I am against those churches/religions that teach false doctrines (traditions of men) *that cover My out stretched saving hands. You blind teachers that teach my children lies that blind them to the truth, the blind leading the blind, to the point that they think their salvation lies in you and not in me* (God). *Do you think you are the one that saves? Ha! I* (God) *am the only one that can save. You fools!"*

God told us 'cursed is the man that trust in a man.' Yet people do it all the time. God said in Jeremiah 4:22, 'My children are Sottish.' Sottish is an Old Saxon word that means 'stupid.' It is God's word, not mine. This is why we came to The Book Ezekiel, Ezekiel 13:20 reads,

"Wherefore thus saith the Lord God; Behold I am against your pillows (coverings)*, where with you there by hunt the souls to make them fly* (away to save their soul)*, and I will tear them* (My children) *from your arms, and will let the souls go* (free them from you with truth)*, even* (including) *the souls that you hunt* (teach them) *to make them fly* (to save their souls).*"*

There you have it. Our Father is against anyone who teaches anyone to fly away in a false hope of gaining salvation. It did not stand with the tower of Babel, and it will not stand this time. Satan, our enemy, knows scripture very well, way better than most men of the cloth. He always has and always will use it against whomever he can.

Well there you have it, THE TRUTH.

What you do with it is your choice. I would be remiss if I did not advise that you keep this book and your Bible very close at hand. The time of the events of the end days are upon us. The sorrows (birth pains) have begun and will not stop. Put on the Gospel armor and prepare for the spiritual fight. It is coming. It has been said that a man (no gender) does what he needs to do until his destiny is revealed, and then he does what he was born to do. Learn and share the truth. Romans 8:31 states.

"If God be for us, who can be against us?"

God Bless you.

ABOUT THE AUTHOR

Ron Cameron lives in Michigan with his wife Beverly on their farm. He is a fresh face who shines a new light on God's word, the Bible. Ron shares with the reader, his gift for making the complicated in God's word understandable.

Having studied for many years under a true Bible Scholar, Ron leads the reader on a journey that positively identifies the antichrist and the events that are leading up to its arrival.

www.ingramcontent.com/pod-product-compliance
Lightning Source LLC
LaVergne TN
LVHW011228080426
835509LV00005B/381